CHANGE CAN BE CHILD'S PLAY

THE RIGHT MINDSET FOR LEADERS IN A WINNING TEAM

YVES VAN DURME

Lannoo
Campus

D/2023/45/69 – ISBN 978 94 014 9102 0 – NUR 800

Text: David Janssens – Het Woordkantoor
Cover design: Armée de Verre Bookdesign
Interior design: Armée de Verre Bookdesign

LannooCampus Publishers is a subsidiary of Lannoo Publishers,
the book and multimedia division of Lannoo Publishers nv.

LannooCampus Publishers
Vaartkom 41 box 01.02   P.O. Box 23202
3000 Leuven   1100 DS Amsterdam
Belgium   The Netherlands

www.lannoocampus.com

CONTENTS

INTRODUCTION

'YOU HAVE TO DRINK LESS COFFEE', my doctor told me. I cursed him thoroughly. Coffee was a lifesaver. Each morning the first coffee of the day was steaming on the table in front of me, almost before I had opened my eyes. And I drank at least another two cups before I could think about setting off for work. And when I arrived at the office, what was my first destination? You've guessed it: the coffee machine. Now, according to the doctor, I should drink no more than two cups a day, with perhaps a shot of decaf in the evening! 'Impossible', I thought, even though I knew that coffee was the cause of my months of stomach pain and sleepless nights. No one – not even me, apparently – likes change. No matter how liberal our ideas, or how much we like a challenge, or how proud we are to see ourselves as cosmopolitan citizens of the world, we all still like something comforting to hold on to. No matter how small that something might be. From an automatic routine for breakfast – with one hand pouring your coffee (yes, I know, I'm at it again!), while the other hand slots a piece of bread into the toaster – to a fixed ritual before going to bed each night – with one hand cleaning your teeth, while the other hand fits your ear plugs to save you from your partner's relentless snoring. Or a thousand and one other things.

It is the same in our professional life: we like the comfort of the familiar. It is not without good reason that we speak about the 'security' of 'permanent employment'. When we apply for a job, we look for 'stable' companies, which have been operating for as long as we can remember and – to the outside world, at least – hardly seem to have changed during all those years. This is certainly the case in Belgium, where working for the government is still one of the most popular career choices. What could be safer than that? Every change on the work floor, in whatever organisation, inevitably encounters resistance. Even if we are not happy in our work, many of us prefer to stay stuck in our 'reliable' rut than to risk trying something new. In 2015, the average level of job satisfaction in Europe was 7.1 out of 10. That might sound a high score, but it isn't. Because it is an average, it means that there are an awful lot of people in Europe who, for whatever reason, are certainly unhappy with their daily occupation. Understandably, this has an influence on their personal happiness and functioning, but it is also, self-evidently, not a good thing for their employers. Nevertheless, the vast majority are content to 'grin and bear it' and very few go in search of new professional opportunities. At the same time, most organisations show the same lack of enthusiasm when it comes to taking measures to improve job satisfaction, effectiveness and efficiency. Because that would require change. And change always hurts.

Even so, change is a necessity. And change is unavoidable. *Panta rhei*, as the pre-Socratic philosopher Heraclitus once said. Everything flows. The only constant is change. And if that is true for metaphysics, it is also true at the more prosaic level of organisations. Some changes take place automatically, almost without being noticed. Others are more intrusive and some are so far-reaching that we speak of a transformation.

Change management steers these processes of change and transformation. Not in an improvised manner, but based on insights that are supported by huge experience and tons of literature. In fact, change management is one of the most widely researched and written-about practices in the organisational domain. So why add yet another book to this already impressive corpus? My answer is simple: because most of these books concentrate on just one vision or school of thought relating to change management, whereas in reality there are many different visions and schools. I do not wish to put all my eggs in one basket, as it were. I prefer to investigate what actually connects all these visions, rather than what separates them. I then test these common factors against what practice has to tell us.

But there is another important reason why I wanted to write this book: change is really not as difficult as it is sometimes portrayed and as we often seem to think. Primarily, change is a question of finding the right mindset, of knowing why you want to change something, how you want to do it, and what exactly you will need to make this possible. The more clearly you can answer these questions, the sooner you will realise that change is really child's play. That is why in the following 180 or so pages I will approach change as though it were a kind of game, just like the family games we all play at home. Sometimes it seems like *The Game of Life*, in which you need to make smart choices at strategic moments to stay on the right path. On other occasions it is more like *Ludo*, where all four pieces are moving forward towards the same destination at the same time. Board games of this kind all have rules that, in theory, need to be followed strictly. But when we land on a 'Free Parking' square during a game of *Monopoly*, many of us are still inclined to pocket the 'fines' money that has accumulated in the centre of the board, even though this is not what the rules say! As far as I am concerned, you can apply this same flexible approach when reading my book. If you want to work your way from cover to cover, no problem! But if you want to cherry pick, or start in the middle and come back to the first half later (or not at all), that's no problem either! Hardly surprising, then, that for the cover of the book we chose an illustration of the world's bestselling board game!

To make things easier, the book has been compiled in the form of a figure of eight, which allows you to jump in at any point. At the same time, a figure of eight also has a pleasing symbolism: it is an endless loop, just like change itself. Every change starts with the question of why you want to change something. Only then can you decide how you want to change things and what you will need to make this possible. Initially, this might seem like walking along a straight road, but in reality it will take you on a twisty-turny course that ultimately brings you back – sometimes after a real rollercoaster of a ride – to the point where you first started: the 'why'. To make sure that you don't get lost along the way, at the beginning of each chapter you will find a map of the figure of eight loop, with an arrow indicating your current position. A bit like on the street maps that you can find in most towns and cities. And just as in *Monopoly* you follow the streets in the direction indicated by the arrow in the 'Start' square, so you do the same with the arrow in our loop. Each part of the loop – in other words, each chapter – starts with a list of questions that will help you to find your way through the change trajectory. There is one question in particular that applies to all change in all organisations: what kind of leader do you want to be? Because change and leadership go hand in hand. A process that does not match your skills as a leader is doomed to failure. Perhaps you are not the right person to lead change in your organisation? Maybe not, but this is not an insurmountable problem – as long as you realise it in good time.

Because playing a game on your own is not much fun (and in the case of *Monopoly* is impossible), I have called on the help of a number of experts to accompany you. You will be able to benefit from their practical knowledge and experience throughout my story. Anyone who has ever played *Dungeons & Dragons* will know that it is dangerous to stay in the dark forests where the trolls live. If you ever find yourself there, you need a good dose of magic to survive. Hopefully, this book will not lead you into a dark forest, but it never does any harm to have a little bit of magic at your disposal. For this reason, the text contains a number of magic cards, which refer you to books that have inspired me over the years. Some of these books come from the world of change management; other come from completely different worlds, but offer alternative points of view on a range of subjects that can be hugely useful during change trajectories.

And how did things work out with my coffee drinking? As soon as I convinced myself that it was all a question of mindset – after all, I am a change manager! – I quickly discovered that this change was also child's play. My doctor is delighted – and I now sleep like a baby!

Why me and not someone else?
—

That's all well and good, I can hear my critical readers thinking, but who the hell is Yves Van Durme to try and thrust his vision on change management down my throat? Who am I? That is a good question – and one that is as difficult to answer as eliminating all those men with glasses, moustaches and beards in a game of *Who Is it?*, so that you can finally find the person you are looking for. Who I am is the result of various change processes I have undergone since the earliest days of my youth. Who we are, what we do and how we think are never static. We are all constantly in change, from cradle to the grave. My particular cradle was in the midst of a family from the Belgian city of Ghent, although it was to be a number of years before I saw much of my 'home town'. When I was just 18 days old, we moved to Mali, where we stayed until I was in nursery school. This was followed by a spell in Burundi, where I followed the first and second years of primary education in Dutch at the Belgian school in Bujumbura, before we moved on again, this time to Yaoundé, the capital city of Cameroon, where my schooling continued in French. This is a lot of adjustment for a child to take on board, but at the time it seemed like the most normal thing in the world. If you grow up in these kinds of circumstances, change becomes part of your daily life. This was something that stood me in good stead later in my professional career. In addition, during our time in Cameroon, we had to live through a failed coup d'état, another experience that stays with you for the rest of your days.

After Yaoundé, our next port of call was a miserable town in the north of Cameroon, where they spoke English. For me, it was strange how the towns in that part of the country were laid out on a strict grid pattern, like the streets in New York, whereas the cities where the French influence was strongest developed in a more random, more organic manner, comparable with the medieval street plans in Western Europe. The same difference was also noticeable in the culture of the local inhabitants. At first glance, they all seemed alike, but when you live amongst them and look more closely, the nuances that distinguish them become more apparent. These differences were more pronounced when it came to their attitude towards foreigners. They showed much more resentment towards Belgians than towards the French, and this because of associations with the colonial past. The French saw their colonialism much more as an emancipatory enterprise than the Belgians. Mixed marriages were allowed and the schools were also mixed. In Belgian colonies, there was greater segregation and relationships between the colonists and the indigenous population were officially forbidden. By seeing these differences as a young child, I learnt early in life to search for the things that connect people, rather than separate them.

From an academic perspective, this was not the most interesting or profitable period of my education. When we lived in northern Cameroon, the

French school in Yaoundé sent me weekly lessons by post that I was able to complete in two or three days, after which I had a very long weekend! But at least I learnt how to speak decent French. From Cameroon, we later relocated to what was then Zaire and is now the Democratic Republic of Congo. In Lubumbashi, I once again found myself in a Belgian college, but still speaking French. I also felt the same colonial resentment against the Belgians that we had experienced before.

" **You can push people to give the best of themselves, but you should never push them over their limits. That is something that I no longer do with myself.**

By now, I was a teenager and my parents thought that it was time to give me a more solid grounding. Consequently, just after my fourteenth birthday, we returned to Belgium, where I soon found myself attending the third year of secondary education at what is now the IVG school in Ghent, where my lessons were once again in Dutch. There was obviously a certain logic in my parents' thinking, but their hopes for me were not wholly fulfilled. All that travelling as a child meant that I could adjust and had no real attachment to any one place, but it also meant that there was nowhere I really felt 'at home' – not even in my native country. I didn't really belong, in part because I was not familiar with (or felt comfortable with) local habits and customs. If I wear a shirt today, it is because I learnt to do so during that period. In Africa, we wore as few clothes as possible and certainly not shirts with the 'right' label. To compensate for this 'out-of-place' feeling, I threw myself into playing sport. I trained 19 hours a week in my efforts to become an even better squash player. Even when I wasn't on court, I spent time analysing my performance right down to the smallest details, searching for that extra one percent that could make all the difference to my game. Why? I had a compulsive desire to prove myself. It was at least one aspect of my life over which I had control.

Because I quickly achieved a higher level, I was asked if I wanted to give squash lessons. It was an interesting offer for a seventeen-year-old in need of some extra cash, but it turned out that I was an awful teacher. With my younger pupils, I had no authority. With my older pupils, I simply gave them bits of my own training, on the assumption that what worked for me would work for them. I soon discovered, however, that 'the harder, the better' was not what everyone needed. Fortunately, there were a few sensible thirty-some-things who said: 'Yves, have you ever asked yourself what we expect to get out of your training?' At first, I didn't understand the question, because in my opinion what I was doing was right. They soon made clear that it was not always my opinion – or my choices – that counted. If I wasn't careful, club members would start to spend their free time differently – and I would lose my nice little earner!

This moment was a turning point for me. The signal that I should learn more about how to give lessons and how people interact with each other was a real eye-opener. I realised for the first time that inter-human relations always need to come first, whatever the context. It was my first (unconscious) experience of change management. Because training, and giving lessons in training, are learning processes that involve constant change. It is not simply a question of constantly trying to perform better, but also of taking account of the ever-variable human factor.

Thanks to sport, I was able to learn about myself through and through. I learnt how to get the best out of myself, but also learnt how to recognise my limits. Because you inevitably make mistakes, and these soon take you over those limits. There were times when this was emotionally challenging, but it was precisely because I went through those difficult moments that in my professional life I now take account of the emotional strain that people are able to bear. You can push people to give the best of themselves, but you should never push them over their limits. That is something that I no longer do with myself. I know myself well and I know what I can do and, most importantly, what I can't do.

After scarcely a year back in Europe, my father was posted to a new job in Tunisia. It was decided that it was better for his wife and children not to accompany him. This meant that I only saw my father five times a year and for the next four years we had to spend our summers in Tunisia, where it was blisteringly hot. It was there that I learnt to watch the Tour de France on television, simply to pass the time. Yet during that same period I also learnt during the cold winter months how to keep a family together. My father wasn't there and my mother was drifting further and further into alcoholism. As the oldest of the three children, it was up to me to take the lead and assume responsibility, whilst also trying to help our mother to free herself from her addiction. This taught me a huge amount about human behaviour. You can cry, beg, threaten and even blackmail an addict, but as long as he or she does not want to 'kick the habit', you will have little or no impact. It was a lesson learnt through bitter personal experience.

This knowledge is something that I still take with me today in all the change trajectories with which I am involved. If people do not want to participate in change, you can move heaven and earth but nothing will persuade them to the contrary. My basic question is always this: what do you really want to achieve, how badly do you want it and how much are you prepared to sacrifice to get it? If company leaders say 'I want to make things better for our organisation', that is a fine and noble objective. But if I then ask them what price they are willing to pay, are they willing to change themselves and will they let go of people who cannot accept the new philosophy, the conversation suddenly becomes more difficult.

After secondary school, I felt that my parents should sponsor me to travel and see the world. Because they couldn't (or wouldn't) agree on the financial aspect, I ended up going to university instead to study medicine. Why? Because I wanted to found a clinic where parents could order their 'ideal' baby (at the time, I was a great fan of science fiction). Not perhaps the best motive in the world for studying medicine and, not surprisingly, I soon lost interest. The course was too long, too boring and I knew that I lacked the necessary self-discipline. My parents still insisted that I should get a diploma of some kind and so I went to study commercial engineering, before later moving on again, this time to the EHSAL management school, where I was given a top-sport status, since I had now trained several junior squash players who had won titles in Belgium and the Netherlands.

Because none of the players I was coaching preferred to put sport ahead of their studies, at the end of the 1990s I decided to move to Malaysia or the United States to become a full-time professional coach. I eventually signed a contract in New York to give lessons to the children of rich parents. American elite schools not only demand academic brilliance, but also sporting excellence. My coaching was designed to ensure the second part of this equation. Soon after, however, I saw an advertisement by De Witte & Morel: the recruitment company were looking for someone who could identify the strengths and weaknesses of candidates in a single day. I wasn't optimistic about my chances but decided to apply anyway. I had a fun day doing the tests and interviews, but thought that would be the end of it. The feedback, when it came, was surprisingly accurate. Even more surprising was the fact that I got the job.

As a qualified commercial engineer, at De Witte & Morel I found myself half-way up the pecking order, somewhere between the clinical psychologists, who were the top of the hierarchical ladder, and the industrial psychologists, who were very much at the bottom. For the next eleven years, I was once again very much the odd man out. I learnt how to identify high potentials: ill-mannered individuals who develop at lightning speed, going from one promotion to the next, usually with an unpleasant degree of arrogance. Unfortunately, they increasingly reminded me of myself... I was just 31 years old and already in the senior management committee. It made me cocky and I regularly clashed with the managing director, Ivan De Witte. One of our confrontations was so fierce that it was impossible to repair the breach between us. I can't remember who was right, but De Witte was the boss and therefore I had to go – but not until eleven months later, because I was locked in financially. For the future, this taught me to make sure to always maintain a sense of independence. If things aren't working out, we part company. That is the independence that I have today at Deloitte's.

At De Witte & Morel, I was concerned primarily with individuals. How can you coach individuals and map out their strengths and weaknesses? We were also interested in HR policy. But for me, it was all too theoretical. All the major consultancy players design structures for people who don't really exist. I wanted to take the organisation and its existing teams as the starting point, to create structures and recipes for change processes. At Deloitte, I now work far more with strategy and organisation, with individuals and how they function in a team. This is a completely different angle of approach.

Even so, in recent years I felt that I wanted and needed something more. To me, the dominant insights in the field of change management feel out-of-date. That is why I have studied the newest theories in great depth and also learnt much from other domains. As a result, I have elaborated a new global vision on change that is not a passe-partout, but is highly dependent on the specific organisation, the wider context and, above all, the people who are responsible for the change. This vision does not always comply with current thinking at Deloitte, but they have allowed me the freedom to further develop my ideas, but with a caveat: show us what you mean and set it down on paper. That is what I have done with this book.

Nelson Mandela
15 LESSONS ABOUT LIFE, LOVE AND LEADERSHIP

It is not always businessmen and women who inspire people the most. Perhaps it has something to do with my youth in Africa, but if I am looking for inspiration I often look no further than Nelson Mandela. After years of imprisonment under the apartheid regime, he attempted to seek the peace and reconciliation that would set South Africa on the path towards a better future. He was a natural leader and a charismatic president. Richard Stengel has written down the most important life lessons of Nelson Mandela in this book. A book that I like to open whenever I am not sure which way to go.

Richard Stengel, Kosmos, 2010

1

WHY

WHY CHANGE (NOW)?

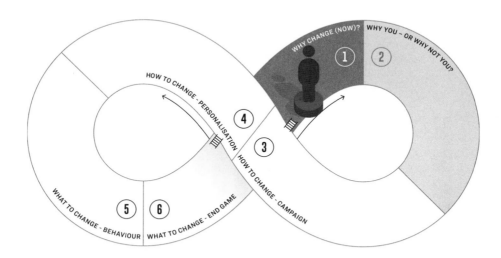

- Can you explain to your mother(-in-law) why you want to change?
- What would you lose and what would you gain with this change?
- What parts of the system will you need to activate to achieve this change?
- Who, at this moment in time, is waiting for change and who is asking for it?
- Are the success criteria for the change clear or measurable?

THE BOX IS OPEN, the *Monopoly* board is spread out on the table and the pieces have been handed out. We can start the game. But why exactly do we play games? Perhaps to kill time? Maybe. A game of patience is useful for that and is marginally less boring than watching paint dry. Usually, however, we play games to entertain ourselves and to seek contact with others. Unfortunately, we often forget this question about why we actually do something. That is a pity, because the 'why' question is an important question, a point that Simon Sinek has underlined in a brilliant manner. Sinek's Golden Circle is a simple leadership model consisting of three circles. These three circles each contain a single word: 'what', 'how' and 'why'. The core of Sinek's creed is: 'start with why'. Why? Because the 'why' lays bare the basic motivation of human action and forms the yardstick for everything that follows. Even so, Sinek argues that while all leaders know what they are doing and some of them know how they are doing it, remarkably few of them know why they are doing it. And in change management it is no different. Everything needs to start with the question of why you want to change. In broad terms, this can usually be explained with reference to external and internal factors.

> **Everything starts with the question of why you want to change. In broad terms, this can usually be explained with reference to internal and external factors.**

If a set of regulations changes, there is not much room for thought. You can have an opinion about the change, but in essence you have to accept that you have a certain amount of time to comply. That is a purely external reason for change. Of course, you can always use an external reason as an excuse for concealing other reasons. You will often hear it said, for example, that a competitor or a customer has 'forced' a company to do something in a particular way. While a competitor or a customer might be in a position to threaten, they are seldom able to force a company to do anything it does not want to do – although it can sometimes be convenient to use this as a justification to hide the real reason for the change. But if you want to offer a customer a completely new method of service provision, you are dealing with a very different form of 'why'. In this case, there is room for thinking about how you want to do this and what is necessary to make it possible.

When you are dealing with the 'why', there are two forces at work. The first is the 'must' factor. Every organisation has a certain hierarchy or power structure that can be used to push through a particular 'why'. This structure

– whether it is weak or strong – gives some people the possibility to say: 'If you don't do this, you will have to suffer the consequences'. In addition, there is also a 'why' that serves as a more positive force, a force that says: 'We need to change in order to make a difference, to do something we can be proud of, to achieve success, to grow together…'

For me, it is difficult not to pass judgement on the nature of the 'why'. Consider, for example, a company in the food sector. You might want to do your utmost to make the world a better place, but if you don't have the necessary food safety certificates you won't be able to produce or do anything. Because you are not in compliance with the relevant regulations. This is a kind of negative 'why' for initiating change. Why is the production process subject to norms and rules? Because that is what the law says: it must be so. And if it is not so, there is no production process. In this case, the 'why' has nothing to do with self-realisation: that is only the case with positive 'whys'. There is also a difference between small 'whys' and big 'whys'. A big 'why' relates back to the fundamental reason for the organisation's existence. This can often be easy to determine, but does not always offer certainty. If Greenpeace asks itself the 'why' question, it is easy for them to find the answer. Their message about how they want to contribute to a better world is abundantly clear. For a bank, however, the situation is less clear-cut. What is a bank? It is an intermediary for the provision of financial services. You can build an attractive story around this raison d'etre, explaining how the bank is there to allow people to realise their dreams in life, and this actually sounds quite good. But it fails to get to the heart of the matter, because it does not say that the bank wants to do this in a manner that will allow it a certain (and significant) margin of profit. In other words, the nature of an organisation's activities sets a filter on the types of 'why' that it can propose.

To find the big 'why', I always like to look at the organisation's complete system, a bit like an anthropologist looks at entire societies. Or the way in which a chess grandmaster has a complete overview of the game and does not just focus on important pieces like the king and queen. If an organisation has lots of managers, both senior and junior, that is generally because the organisation wants it that way. This is often the result of a cost-saving reasoning on the part of the CEO. Each manager is encouraged to save more than the manager above him and each new manager must save more than his predecessor. If you create new levels of subordinate managers, this means that the responsibility for cost-saving can be shifted. It becomes easier to justify yourself to the manager above you, if you have two managers below you who need to justify themselves to you. At the same time, I have often been struck by how seldom organisations make full use of their entire system. Every organisation is subject to a permanent process of change. Why? Because creative people are constantly thinking up alternatives to review the model. Let's look again at an example from the food sector. Imagine that you make the best biscuits in your region and build up a success story on this basis. Suddenly, biscuits from a neighbouring region that are as good as (if not better than) yours break into your market. When this happens, you need to respond creatively – and adjust. This is also the case when tastes change. For many years, we in the West have been eating sweeter and sweeter. As a result, biscuits needed to contain more and more sugar. But now that trend has been reversed, so that consumers are no longer interested in all that unhealthy sugar. So what do you do? Stubbornly persist with your recipe for the best biscuit in the region and watch your turnover fall? Or creatively search for a better alternative recipe?

The way in which that constant change manifests itself depends on the nature of the organisation. Consider, for example, an organisation staffed largely by volunteers, like the Red Cross. The objective of the Red Cross can justifiably be described as noble and for many of its volunteers that noble objective is a decisive motivating factor. For this reason, the process of change in a volunteer organisation offers some interesting lessons, because you cannot realistically appeal to the 'must' factor. The balance of power in the hierarchy is different. It is much more difficult to tell volunteers that they must do this or that. If they don't want to, they will just withdraw their support. With a bank, the situation is almost completely the reverse. For a start, there is much less room for the formulation of a noble objective. The focus is primarily on improving people's quality of life or supporting entrepreneurship, but these objectives are always in balance with the desire to make profit (not that there is nothing wrong with this, of course). In these circumstances, it is also far from easy to introduce change. Are you going give it positive emphasis or a negative one, based on the needs of the organisation and the need for profit? Or both? And if so, how do you strike the right balance?

One of the most important reasons for change in recent decades has been the rapidly increasing pace of technological advancement. How could it be otherwise? Companies need to adjust almost continually or else risk being left behind. This sounds almost self-evident, but in practice it is not always as easy as it sounds. This was something experienced by my good friend and former colleague Alix Rombouts, when he took up a position as HR manager in a Belgian family-run company that is a world player in its sector: 'Before I started in a family company, I assumed that change in the wider world would always filter through to the business world. I soon discovered that this is not the case. I have still got the notes that I made during my first meeting with the management team and I promised myself that I would always keep them as an illustration of how inward-looking even a global organisation can some-times be. There was not the slightest suggestion that these people understood the need for change. On the contrary, the management was confident that it could carry on in the same way for years and still make money. "Digitalisation is nothing for us," they told me, quite literally. On this point, the family was adamant. It was not until another external factor – COVID-19 – dramatically changed the situation that this conviction was undermined. The corona crisis forced us to approach a whole range of matters in a different way. The moment had finally come for us to digitalise.'

In addition to the tension between internal and external factors, the 'why' of change is also subject to a clash of two other extremes: preventative change versus curative change. Preventative change is implemented before it is really necessary. If water were to leak through the hole in our roof, this might lead to damage. So it is better to repair or replace the roof while the weather is good and before it rains. If we delay for too long and it subsequently pours down for weeks on end, it will be too late to take remedial action. By pointing out the possibility of this extreme scenario, you stimulate an organic process, comparable with giving a plant fertiliser to help it blossom and flourish. On the other side of the coin we find curative change. Why should we repair or re-place our leaking roof? We can simply put a bucket under the hole to catch the water. Or two buckets, if necessary. As long as our building is not completely flooded, there is no real need for change. This kind of extreme possibility is more like pruning a plant hard to correct its growth. When it comes, the change is often driven by personal insights. Why do I want to see something changed? Is it because I want to be ahead of the game or to prevent a looming problem becoming more serious? Or is it because I have no other choice and am almost being swamped by a problem I can no longer control? In this latter eventuality, you will be faced with a so-called 'burning platform', but this can actually be positive for getting things done in a crisis. This was evident, for example, in the approach to the corona crisis. The democratic process was pushed to one side and privacy rights were largely ignored – and the majority of people simply accepted it. Why? Because the building was on fire! In a burning platform situation, there is no question of consulting everyone's opinion or holding endless discussions to draw up a step-by-step plan. You either already have a plan or you send people to every floor in the building to tell them to get out as quickly as possible. A burning platform seldom brings out the best in people, because situations of that kind appeal to our primeval instincts: fight, flight or freeze.

Curative change is also painful. If an untrained muscle suddenly needs to start working, you will feel it the next day. And the day after that. And so on. If you persist, the muscle will eventually become strained. It is the same with change. Organisations that are repeatedly forced into change feel constant pain. Preventative change can relieve or even avoid the strain. So the message is this: evaluate your situation continually, without falling into the trap of perfectionism. Remember that 'good' is often good enough. Check as a team to see what worked well during the last period and try to strengthen it, not least because those are the things that also usually give you most pleasure. Focus the change exclusively on those elements that are not working well or suddenly cause problems. For many organisations, learning how to cope with change in today's world is a serious challenge. We do not know what will change or when it will happen, but we do know that its coming is inevitable and that there will probably be a lot of it. We also know – or should know – that the speed with which change can be implemented and pushed through offers a huge competitive advantage. It is impossible to predict the future, particularly in a volatile and competitive environment, but responding quickly to external events will always give you a massive lead over your slower rivals. This was also evident during the corona epidemic. Nobody could see this crisis coming, but some organisations showed themselves to be more adaptable than others. Being prepared is more than half the battle.

BURNING PLATFORM – The floor is lava

The origin of the term 'burning platform' in a business context dates back to an incident that took place on 6 July 1988, the day on which the Piper Alpha oil rig exploded in the North Sea. This was caused by a failure to check the oil platform's systems properly. After years without a single problem, attention to safety procedures gradually relaxed, with disastrous consequences. The explosion caused an uncontrollable fire, with flames shooting high into the sky. This inferno was visible hundreds of kilometres from the rig and cost 167 oil workers their lives. Initially, the workers locked themselves into a separate section of the rig, hoping (in vain) that the fire would burn itself out. However, three of the workers saw that the situation was hopeless and fled to the edge of the drilling platform. There, they were faced with a terrible choice: between the red-hot flames behind them and the ice-cold water ahead of them. Two of the men opted for the water and jumped to what seemed like certain death. Miraculously, however, they were rescued from the sea in the nick of time. The third man decided to stay on the platform, but was sadly consumed by the fire before the helicopter could reach him.

In change management, the 'burning platform' idiom is used as a metaphor to show that staying where you are is not an option. A burning platform can be caused by both internal and external factors or can even be deliberately created by the organisation's leaders. Whatever its origins, the result is an acute crisis situation, in which options are limited, every decision is challenging and irreversible, and every action carries a high risk of failure. If an organisation is well and truly on fire, change is the only way out, even if that change will be unavoidably painful. Standing still and doing nothing is simply not possible. Because the floor under your feet is lava.

Everyone is better than average

One factor that must always be kept in mind when trying to determine the 'why' of change is human bias. There is always a reference frame and this frame must be kept in sharp focus. Are you looking at the situation with an internal focus or an external focus? The best way to become a world champion is to redefine your definition of the 'world'. Is it your city, village, district or even your own home? In that case, it is not so difficult to be the best at something. I still can remember how, when I was a student, I was able to beat all my friends easily at *Magic: The Gathering*, a fantasy card game full of dragons, trolls and other monsters. I thought that I was unbeatable – until the day I took part in a real *Magic* tournament. Full of confidence, I played my usual Shivan Dragon, only to find that three moves later I had lost the game. Knocked out in the first round! It is no different for organisations and companies. Who or what are you going to compare yourself with? Widening your field of vision takes courage, because only looking at yourself and remaining a big fish in a small pond is much easier and much more enjoyable than trying to swim in the deep ocean, where predators are always on the prowl and your weaknesses will become more apparent.

The change process also requires you to look further than how much change you can realistically achieve within your organisation. Research into change has consistently shown that most changes are not as successfully implemented as planned. Exactly how successful they are is something that is difficult to measure, not only because the relevant statistical parameters are extremely complex, but also because success is largely a matter of perception. Once again, human bias plays a role. If you ask a hundred people whether or not they are a better than average driver, 80 percent of them will say that they are – which is, of course, statistically impossible. It is no different in change management. A similar survey would show that 80 percent of managers think that they are better than average at implementing change, whereas the statistics suggest that in reality the opposite is true, particularly when it comes to complex change relating to culture – and this while cultural change is one of the most frequently desired aspects of organisational planning! We want a customer-oriented culture, or a culture of discipline, or even in more recent years a culture of compliance, focused on following the rules religiously in all branches of our activities.

Wanting to change your organisational culture almost borders on the schizophrenic. As a rule, people only have a single personality – thankfully! – and this personality determines how they deal with different situations. In much the same way, organisations have a dominant culture, which finds expression in everything that the organisation does. Whoever wishes to change that culture, even in part, obviously regards it as a problem. If the personality of an individual is seen as a problem, this is viewed as a crisis situation, the most common solutions for which are the temporary removal of that person from society or subjecting him/her to years of remedial therapy. Yet again, it is the same for organisations. An organisation with a problematic culture faces a fundamental challenge. To make it sound less serious and wide-ranging, it is customary in the business world to talk of 'mindset' rather than culture. Mindset is what influences your behaviour at moments when no one else is looking. Is that behaviour very different, just a little different or no different at all from your behaviour when someone from the hierarchy is looking? Or to put it in game terms: are you someone who takes a sneaky look at the cards of your distracted opponent when playing *Stratego* or are you Mr (or Mrs) Squeaky Clean, who would never dream of doing such a thing? It is important to take this into account during cultural change. Is the planned change a change where the moments of truth will be directed by the hierarchy or are there plenty of moments when this direction is lacking, so that the mindset of the employees comes more strongly into play as the determining factor for behaviour? These two scenarios require different kinds of change.

Let's imagine that you want a customer-oriented culture. The first question you need to ask is: how many customer interactions are there? If you sell televisions, there are two: the moment of sale and the moment of installation. Or perhaps three, if your customer has initial doubts. This means that it is always possible for the hierarchy to be present in these moments. It is a different story if your activity involves continuous customer interaction. That makes it impossible for the hierarchy to be constantly involved. Even if it could be, that would be guaranteed to destroy your customer-orientation in no time at all: no customer wants every question and every contact referred back to the hierarchy, since that suggests a lack of trust and competence. However, most organisations are still developed in keeping with a logic based on efficiency and the avoidance of errors. This so-called Taylorian thinking, named after Frederick Taylor, transforms people into machines and relies on the belief that all processes in an organisation are controllable. The starting premise for these organisations is: what is the end product? If the output is strictly defined, you can shape your processes and therefore your people so that everything serves this all-important output. Whether or not this is really desirable is another matter, but it is nonetheless the case that most organisations (consciously or less consciously) make use of this method.

TAYLORISM: FOUR PRINCIPLES TO REMEMBER – OR FORGET

As the founder of scientific management, the American Frederick Taylor (1856–1915) was one of the most influential figures in the industrial thinking of the 20th and 21st centuries. Taylor was an engineer who was fascinated by mechanical processes and wanted to apply them to labour and human behaviour. In this respect, he was also a child of his time. His book, *The Principles of Scientific Management*, was published in 1911, a moment in time when the nature of working conditions was not the most important concern. *Taylorism* reached its high-water mark during the Great Depression and was mocked by Charlie Chaplin in his classic film *Modern Times* (1936). Taylor's starting point was a simple one: workers are structurally lazy, which threatens the efficiency of production. His solution was an all-embracing control system that reduced the workers to automatons. Each worker had to be programmed to implement a series of repetitive actions, which kept the possibility of error to a minimum. As if this were not enough, the system was also subjected to a constant process of analysis and revision, making it ever more efficient, until the workers themselves also worked like machines. To achieve this optimal efficiency, Taylor recommended the application of the following four principles:

1   Use scientific methods to determine and standardise the best way to perform each task.
2   Define tasks and responsibilities clearly.
3   Pay higher wages to the best performing workers.
4   Create a clear hierarchy of authority and control workers strictly.

It sounds simply enough, but is it also healthy? Reducing people to the level of machines means eliminating their emotions. However, this does not work, because people are not the wholly rational beings that Taylorism presupposes. The majority of the decisions we take are based on a combination of reason and emotion, or often just the latter. For this reason, strict Taylorism is not only degrading and inhuman, but also has little value as a theory. Models about people and the economy only became interesting from the moment in history when psychologists first won the Nobel Prize for Economics.

> ❞ Models about people and the economy only became interesting from the moment in history when psychologists first won the Nobel Prize for Economics.

If you really want your thinking to become customer-oriented, you need to have variation in your interactions. Customers in the 21st century are no longer happy with standard answers to every question. Unfortunately, this wish often conflicts with the work practices of many of today's organisations, which have not moved on much since Henry Ford made his famous comment about the first mass produced car in the early 1900s: 'The Ford T is available in all colours, as long as it is black'. To stay with cars, customers today not only expect to choose the colour, but also the interior fabric, the style and covering of the seats, the wheel hubs, etc., etc. And the more choice options you give, the more complex your organisation and its operations become. Which is really an elegant way to say that there are more points at which you and your organisation can get things wrong.

This goes against the Taylorian logic that everything should be done to eliminate mistakes and is therefore at odds with the prevailing culture in many organisations. In this way, the organisations in question eventually arrive at the need for change. Another important factor is the internet. This has turned everything upside down in recent years. Because so much information is now instantly available to consumers, the television seller we mentioned earlier not only needs to take account of the choice options of his 'physical' high street competitors, but also of his new online rivals. Nowadays, remarkably enough, it often happens that the customer is better informed than the professional he is dealing with!

An interesting concept in this respect is the idea of good and bad complexity. An example of bad complexity is when a customer is not impressed because he finds his product almost impossible to unpack, because of the amount and the design of the packaging. An example of good complexity is when the design and opening of the packaging is a positive experience in itself. In both cases, the product can be almost identical, but the difference in the packaging also leads to the product being perceived differently. Apple, for instance, is famed for its stylish packaging, which is part and parcel of the brand's allure. When they buy a mobile phone, most people throw away the packaging, but not if they buy an Apple. The next step in the good complexity process is to ensure that people are willing to pay more for the experience it provides. In essence, this means that you want them to pay more for the way the product is packed. It is interesting to reflect on how this choice was made. Apple's packaging does not provide better product protection than its rivals, is not more environmentally friendly, and is not a response to specific legislation. In other words, in this case the 'why' is a purely internal option – and also a good example of the value of sometimes moving away from the idea that the product and the production process should be the sole central factors in the organisation's thinking.

The spectrum of change
—

Like almost everything else in life, change has a broad spectrum of complexity. As already mentioned, context also plays an important role. Taken together, these two factors form a reality check in the 'why' phase. Within the change spectrum, you will be confronted with simple problems and complex problems, as well as known and unknown solutions. A simple problem might be something like the need to comply with food safety regulations, which say that certain steps must be taken to comply with certain norms. This is a clear problem with a clear answer. Another example might be integrating a smaller company into a large organisation. This is a wider-ranging situation, involving more elements that may make things more complicated, but in essence it remains a simple problem, because all the answers are known, such as the existence of different systems to harmonise all the necessary financial and core activities. Culture is also a known phenomenon, yet even though cultures are certainly more difficult to integrate, once again you will largely be dealing with known variables. With complex problems, you enter a whole new world, where you know none of the answers. Starting a new activity is a good example. Imagine that you want to allow your customers to design their own clothes, for which you will then provide the production process. This requires you to enter a completely unknown environment, where the solutions will also be unknown.

There are many degrees of difficulty between simple and complex problems. Some problems are simple to solve, perhaps on the basis of a guideline or a measure that is clear and obvious. A combination of simple problems can also often be dealt with on the basis of a range of simple solutions. But if the solutions are unknown, things become much more complicated. And at the extreme end of this spectrum we find the dream of every change manager: wicked problems. If you are faced by a wicked problem, you would be well advised to get your old box of *Dungeons & Dragons* out of the cellar, because without your magic hat there is no way you will ever find a solution! A problem is defined as wicked if it fails to conform to any of the other standard definitions. In other words, wicked problems are unique and, perhaps for this reason, they have a tendency to slip through your hands. They can also be a symptom of other problems and their solutions are not good or bad, but rather right or wrong, although their outcomes do not immediately lend themselves to testing. Most crucially, they only offer you a single, one-off chance to get things right.

The complexity axis is also influenced by the second axis in the change spectrum: the extent to which an organisation is capable of organising its change. An organisation that is searching for a scapegoat to blame for the situation in which it finds itself will soon switch into discussion mode, even for simple problems. In this case, the organisation probably has a dysfunctional leadership team that is not able to set the necessary priorities. This prioritising is a serious challenge in many organisations. If there is only a single simple

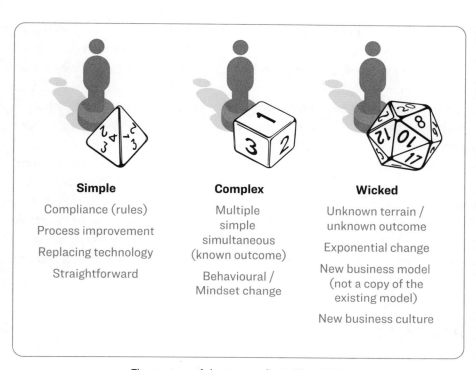

Simple	Complex	Wicked
Compliance (rules)	Multiple simple simultaneous (known outcome)	Unknown terrain / unknown outcome
Process improvement		Exponential change
Replacing technology		New business model (not a copy of the existing model)
Straightforward	Behavioural / Mindset change	New business culture

The spectrum of change according to Horst Rittel

problem to be solved, there should be enough clever people around in any organisation to make this possible. If, however, there are a number of simple or less simple problems and you are not able to solve them all at the same time, this makes necessary the setting of priorities. This, in turn, is linked to the extent to which your organisation is able to cope with change or, alternatively, is already suffering from change fatigue. Without naming any names, I know of a company where, for example, the timing of change is not regarded as a priority. They start with the idea of completing a trajectory in three months, but it actually takes them six months. Or four years instead of two years. For them, the timing is of secondary importance. What counts is doing things right and not making any mistakes. As a result, time is a variable with which they are prepared to be flexible. This is what determines their capacity for change: not succeeding in achieving objectives within the projected time. Because if you say that you are achieving objectives, but with a much greater delay than was planned, you are not really achieving at all.

What is involved here is not just the variables, but also the organisation's past history. An organisation can have a history of achieving all its objectives on time, but it can also be an organisation that pushes through change at all costs, even to the extent of exhausting its workforce. Or, alternatively, an organisation where the workforce can see the benefit of change for themselves. This latter possibility is interesting. A change that feels meaningful for employees, improves their well-being, and reduces the pressure they are under at work generates energy. It gives people the feeling: 'I was tired, but now I am interested in my job again and feel full of beans!' This energy balance is something that leaders can use to their advantage in their change design. It is very different in situations where the main concern is to find a scapegoat. In these circumstances, the attitude of the workforce is more likely to be: 'Change? Okay, bring it on – but show me first that you believe in it yourself. If you can convince me, I might be willing to play along...'

The inside track to efficiency
—

The first step in bringing about change is to give people more responsibility. Consider, for example, the running of a hotel reception desk. In one hotel, guests are never given an immediate answer to their questions, because the desk clerk always has to first refer back to her boss. Answering questions on her own initiative is not something that is included in her job description. In a second hotel, just around the corner, a script has been prepared to answer the most frequently asked questions, and perhaps even a few not so frequently asked ones that have occurred in the past. In other words, the receptionist in this hotel is given more responsibility. In which hotel is the receptionist most likely to become frustrated with their work? More importantly: in which hotel will the guests feel that they are being treated well, so that they are more likely to return and/or recommend it to friends? But even if the two receptionists have different levels of responsibility, there is not much difference between them when it comes to levels of autonomy. Their position is similar to the players in *The Game of Life*, where everyone thinks that they are making their own choices – to marry, to have children, and so on – whereas in reality it is the board that decides for you. The script of the second receptionist is just as tightly defined by the hierarchy as the answers that the first receptionist has to go and find from her boss.

The difference, of course, is in the perception of the people involved. Which brings us back to mindset. In both hotels, efficiency and the avoidance of mistakes are a priority. But they seek to achieve this priority in different ways. In the first hotel, double-checking is important, with slower customer service as a result. In the second hotel, the checking is made in advance, during the preparation of the script. The risk of errors is perhaps slightly greater, but the speed of service delivery is also faster. The basis for these different approaches is, as so often, a different style of leadership. Giving people responsibility can be described as a 'humanistic' approach: if you allow people to develop, society will flourish. This is diametrically opposed to the more authoritarian approach, where the boss is the boss and 'orders are orders'.

How disruptive is change? Up to a certain point, people need patterns in order to be able to perform efficiently. If, however, the pattern becomes automatic, this is when they start to make mistakes, because they no longer need to think about what they are doing. The aim is therefore to reach a point at which people have the technical aspects of their job perfectly under control, so that they can complete the process faultlessly, whilst at the same time keeping the process sufficiently new and challenging, so that they need to remain alert. Consider, for example, driving a car. This is something that is quite hard to learn: two or three pedals at your feet, six gears to manipulate, never mind the switches for lights, windscreen wipers and all the rest. During your first lessons, all you think about (consciously) is: 'What do I have to do next?' Eventually, however, you reach a point where you no longer need to think about the driving, but focus instead on matters like what music you want to hear on the radio. In short, you have reached the point of over-confidence – and this can be dangerous, both for you and for others. And it is exactly the same in organisations and companies. It costs lots of energy and lots of other things as well to reach a point where processes, interactions and production are all optimal, but it requires even greater effort to maintain that situation. Once you have reached this optimal level, there is a danger that nothing more will change, so that the balance actually starts to deteriorate, without you even noticing it. A timely change of mindset can help organisations to avoid this pitfall.

> **" It costs lots of energy and lots of other things as well to reach a point where processes, interactions and production are all optimal, but it requires even greater effort to maintain that situation.**

It is almost perverse to say it, but organisations that take no steps to prevent their comfort zone from becoming a zone of complacency are fertile ground for ambitious change managers. Why? Because it is part of human nature to search for solutions yourself. But it does not work. Imagine that you have been performing the same task for years, while everything in the world around you is changing. There is a strong likelihood that you will try to find alternative ways to do your work more efficiently. In theory, this is an 'attack' on the organisation's agreed processes and such behaviour can often be punished. In reality, however, it is a missed opportunity for improvement. This means that people in the hierarchy are constantly faced with an important choice: do you leave room for the initiation of minor changes from 'inside', to keep the efficiency of the organisation at the desired level, or do you turn every so often to external advisers to view the situation with a neutral eye, because your efficiency levels have been falling? Most leaders still prefer the second option.

Let us return briefly to the food industry. This is an industry where the right cooking time is essential, if you wish to achieve efficient production. However, society's focus is currently on food safety and the reduction of waste, particularly of packaging. Consumers are increasingly irritated if the food they buy in the supermarket is available in multiple packagings, but have no interest in how efficiently that food is produced. Very few food producers are prepared to tackle this change challenge. Curiously enough, however, the processes that aim to achieve waste reduction are also processes that can increase efficiency.

These two objectives are perfectly compatible. The question is this: who needs to take the responsibility? Is it the people who are involved with the processes day after day? Or is it the external advisers, who view the processes with a neutral eye? This is a question that is applicable to every change: does the change come from within the system or from without?

The person behind the worker

With the 'why', the link with psychology is never very far away. As a leader, it is essential to consider what the consequences might be for yourself and for others by changing (or not changing). What will you achieve? How will the change affect people? What impact will it have? If you want something badly, but know that it can only be realised at the expense of others, you will probably continue to want it just as badly, but hopefully you will reflect on the fact that your 'why' is not so innocent and that you also need to draw up a balance of your own loss or gain. Yet even today, the insight that psychology has a place in the business world and certainly in the field of change management is still not universally accepted and understood. As we have seen, the business world was dominated for many years by the influence of Frederick Taylor and his theory of scientific management, and in some parts of the economy that is still the case. It took almost a century before organisations began to devote serious attention to the person behind the worker. An interesting study of this evolution from mechanical to more self-steering organisations can be found in the book *Reinventing Organisations*, written by the Belgian author Frederic Laloux.

Until the start of this century, the idea of charting the relationship between psychology and economics would have been almost unthinkable. This only began to change following the award in 2002 of the Nobel Prize for Economics – or to give it its proper title, the Sveriges Riksbank Prize in Economic Sciences in Memory of Alfred Nobel – to Daniel Kahneman. This Israeli psychologist integrated insights from his own discipline into the economic sciences, with a particular focus on human judgement and the taking of decisions in situations of uncertainty. Since then, the interconnectedness of psychology and economics has slowly filtered through to large sections of the business community, although the influence of Taylorism is still evident in a number of essential areas. Reward, for example, is an important element in every formal agreement between a worker and an organisation. However, the evolution of reward forms part of an informal agreement, because it is subject to many different expectations and perceptions. In this respect, the human factor plays a defining role. If, when you are playing *Monopoly*, you have a hotel on Trafalgar Square, you attach a subjective value to this situation and, at first, will probably be satisfied with it. But if, later on, another player has a hotel on Mayfair, you will probably be a lot less satisfied, even though both hotels cost just as much to buy.

Rewards work in the same way. Our inclination to compare makes things difficult. The key question is who should we compare ourselves with? This is purely subjective – which brings us back to our 80 percent of car drivers who think that they are better than average. The huge majority of workers also think that they perform better than their colleagues and therefore logically also think that they should earn more. This makes the evolution of a fair reward system very difficult, because perception will always be pivotal. For this reason, there is a great temptation for organisational leaders to use the evolution of rewards as an instrument of power. They argue that if fairness – or a perception of fairness – is not possible, then it makes good economic sense to use rewards as a way to influence their workers' behaviour. Consider, for instance, the following example. On board an aircraft, there are two kinds of personnel: those who ensure that the aircraft takes off and lands safely, and those who try to make the flying experience a pleasant one. As far as the first group is concerned, it is important not to have huge differences in terms of quality and competence. No airline wants a good pilot on one plane and a bad pilot on another plane. You just want good pilots. Even a super-pilot, who can make his plane perform all kinds of aerobatic tricks, offers you no added value: you are only interested in his ability to fly the plane safely from point A to point B. This means that as an airline it makes sense not to use rewards to create variation and stimulate difference. If you were to give your pilots pay increases to encourage them to become better pilots, their desire to demonstrate this improvement would result in much more adventurous – but also much less safe – flights, which might not be appreciated by the majority of your paying customers!

The situation is different with cabin personnel. A friendly smile can help to add colour to the flying experience. The reaction of a steward or stewardess after a spilt cup of coffee can influence a passenger either positively or negatively. In other words, variation in behaviour is possible. Cabin crew also earn less than the cockpit crew. Consequently, in their case variation in reward can be used to stimulate the right behaviour. For example, a measurable level of customer satisfaction could be used to give the cabin crew a bonus. But this system would not work for, say, civil servants employed by the state. Most of these officials work hard and do a good job, but that makes little or no difference, because their salary scales are statutorily fixed, so that everyone with the same grade and the same number of years of service gets the same amount of pay at the end of the month. As a result, rewards cannot be used by the state to encourage people to evolve in what they are doing. Other levers will therefore be necessary to motivate and stimulate people, so that they do not slip out of their comfort zone and into the zone of complacency.

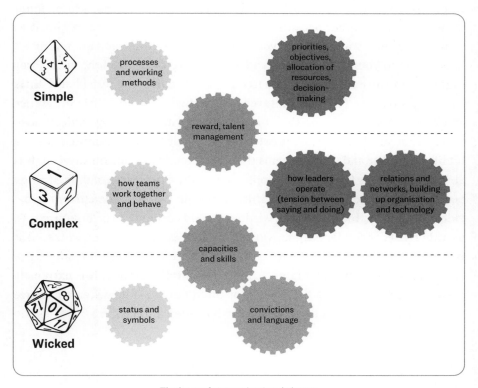

The levers for organisational change

Internal competition is one such lever, which is particularly effective on men. This instrument – and the promise of promotion it brings – helps to keep people on their toes at work, but there is a risk that it may lead to excesses and the cutting of corners by ambitious employees, who want to be the fastest to produce the best end results. For that reason, this method is only useful for production processes where the number of error-free units made or transactions performed is central. For activities that require more thought, internal competition is less appropriate. How many good ideas can you dream up in a minute? This simple question proves the obvious absurdity of this notion. Even so, there are many organisations where internal competition is still encouraged for creative functions.

In addition to formal levers like rewards, there are also a number of informal levers that can be employed. These tend to be associated with the organisational culture. For example, in one organisation, you know that it is smart to keep your crazy ideas to yourself; otherwise your colleagues and superiors will make you a laughing stock – a situation that many people will be familiar with. Or, in another organisation, it is smart to keep your crazy ideas to yourself, because you know that you will be expected to develop them yourself in addition to your normal work and will be judged accordingly. In this way, organisations use informal levers to ensure that colouring outside the lines will be 'punished'. For the employees concerned, it makes little difference whether their employers do this consciously or not. On the downside, it does, however, mean that it becomes extremely difficult to change mindset. It is a bit like in traditional tribal systems that are strongly focused on survival. It is almost impossible for younger people to introduce new ways of doing things, because their ancestors did everything a certain way and the current tribal elders insist that this traditional wisdom should continue to be honoured. To do otherwise, the elders argue, would be madness and, almost worse, lacking in respect. I mentioned earlier that there are two kinds of change: preventative and curative. Changing a culture or mindset curatively is extremely difficult, because it takes time, which is often not available when a curative remedy is needed, and it takes trust, which is often also lacking.

There has to be well-being
—

Under the influence of new social trends, in recent years organisations have devoted more and more attention to well-being. This does not mean, however, that they make systematic use of the findings of Daniel Kahneman and others to promote the welfare of their people. True, during the corona crisis the level of attention to employee well-being reached new heights, but this was primarily a question of physical health and hygiene. There was much less concern for mental health. Nevertheless, both types of health – physical and mental – are of vital importance. We are all familiar with Maslow's pyramid of human needs. The bottom levels deal with purely physical needs, safety and security. The top level deals with the need for self-realisation. If you look at the average day of someone in the Western world, you can – hopefully – divide it up into eight hours sleep, eight hours work and eight hours of relaxation. Very few people derive meaning in their life from sleep, so that meaning will have to come from that other key element in their daily existence: work. This means that during the performance of that work it is not only crucial to guarantee the physical health of the workforce, but also their psychological health. This requires that organisations pay attention to all aspects of well-being.

Unfortunately, in most organisations the attention given to mental well-being is largely curative: it is only when problems arise that guidance and possible solutions are considered. A preventative policy that regards well-being as a benefit to be actively pursued is rare. Which is curious, because we all have good and bad days. On good days, you probably have a greater desire to work and are able to do more than usual. But on bad days, your motivation is low and the amount of work you complete is reduced. This is a feeling that everyone in every job has at one time or another, so it makes sense for organisations to try and cut out (or at least cut down) the number of these bad days. Nevertheless, there are very few companies prepared to make the necessary effort, by including a preventative welfare policy in their rules and regulations. The main reason for this is that the business world still has a strong focus on units of time. Work is always related to time; in particular, hours.

That being said, devoting attention to mental well-being is far from evident in some situations. Consider the case of two storemen working in a warehouse. One strictly follows all the rules and can therefore be positively influenced; for example, by the playing of relaxing music. You could even measure his stress levels with a heart rate monitor and adjust the conditions in the warehouse accordingly. In this way, you will end up with an employee who probably feels fit and well, but bears no responsibility whatsoever. The second storeman determines his own route around the warehouse, which is more difficult than just following the standard guidelines. This involves making decisions and decisions mean more stress. On a bad day, the second worker's performance of his duties will be more seriously affected than the work of his rule-compliant colleague. You could assist the mental health of the second worker by positioning the products in the warehouse in such a way that they are easiest to find along his preferred route. But what if a different storeman with different preferences is working in the warehouse the next day? You can hardly reposition the products every 24 hours! The expense would be huge, with no way of justifiably passing on the cost to the customer, because he or she is not really bothered whether the man taking the product off the warehouse shelf was feeling good that day or not.

Once again, the key question resolves around where ultimate responsibility for these issues should lie. Since the time of the Industrial Revolution, significant progress in the field of employee welfare has been made. Lord Lever, the founder of the major British company that would later become Unilever, built the model village of Port Sunlight, to house the workers in his factories in relatively healthy and hygienic conditions. Lady Lever even placed her own art collection in a museum designed to provide 'moral upliftment' for the workforce and their families. In Belgium, companies like Agfa-Gevaert, Solvay and Chemie Tessenderlo have been implementing a similarly paternalistic approach for decades, with their employees living almost in the shadow of the factory chimneys. In the 21st century, the evolution of welfare policy has moved another stage forward, so that it is no longer acceptable for employers to 'interfere' in the private lives of their employees. This also removes the responsibility: employers can still influence the sleep quality of their employees, but are no longer responsible for it. However, this then leads on to a further ethical discussion about how far it is appropriate for an employer to have any concern for the welfare and well-being of employees in matters of this kind, since it inevitably impinges on their private lives in one way or another.

Whatever the pros and cons of this and other similar arguments, it is incontestable that well-being remains an essential factor when considering the 'why' for change. Is that well-being neutral? And in which direction will the change move it? A positive direction or a negative one? This brings us back to the centre of Sinek's Golden Circle: why are we doing what we are doing? When change is being discussed, it is self-evident that an organisation needs to ask itself how it will benefit, but asking what benefits can be gained in respect of well-being should also be a crucial part of this. Increasing workforce availability and improving job satisfaction? These are important values to add to the equation when assessing the choice for change.

> **Increasing workforce availability and improving job satisfaction? These are important values to add to the equation when assessing the choice for change.**

Then there is also the important question of commitment. Research into employee satisfaction has proven a clear link between commitment – a willingness to do more than the standard package of tasks detailed in your job description – and the extent to which the purpose of the organisation – the things for which it stands – is perceived as being 'noble'. One of the most noble industries is the pharmaceutical industry, because it relates directly to people's quality of life. However, studies show that the level of commitment in pharmaceutical companies is not particularly high. This has much to do with the size of these companies. When employees feel that they are only a very small cog in a very big machine, their level of commitment falls. They no longer feel that they are contributing very much to the noble objectives of the sector as a whole.

Are you familiar with classic cartoon of President John F. Kennedy, who asks a cleaner mopping the floor at NASA precisely what he is doing? The cleaner replies: 'I'm helping to put a man on the moon!' Commitment doesn't get any stronger than that! But even if the cleaner had not had the feeling that he was contributing to a higher goal, his answer would still have been correct. In both cases, he was cleaning and its usefulness remains the same. Once again, it is all a matter of mindset. It is the task of the leaders in an organisation to ensure that mindset and purpose are properly aligned with each other, so that the commitment and self-esteem of the workforce can be enhanced. The more noble the personnel regard the 'why', the greater the likelihood that you will be able to engage them more easily in change. That sounds logical, but it is up to you as a leader to make sure that your people do regard your 'why' as noble.

> **It is the task of the leaders in an organisation to ensure that mindset and purpose are properly aligned with each other, so that the commitment and self-esteem of the workforce can be enhanced.**

The effect of enhancing commitment is greater than increasing rewards. Whoever gets an annual pay increase will be happy, and will perhaps work harder for an initial period, but this effect soon fades away. A higher amount on your monthly pay slip may make you euphoric the first time you see it, but less so the second time and not at all the third time. It simply becomes normal. In other words, the effect does not run synchronously with the frequency of the instrument. The increase in annual pay has an impact for three months, but there are still another nine months of the year to go – and further interim pay rises are out of the question. In short, the effort-return ratio is completely out of balance. If you play *Uno*, you usually have a winner after five minutes. The pleasure of winning is limited and wears off very quickly. If you play *Risk*, the pleasure of victory after two or three hours of effort is greater, but you probably get as much (if not more) satisfaction from the plans and strategies you executed during the game. In other words, the pleasure of playing takes precedence over the pleasure of winning, just as greater job satisfaction takes precedence over pay increases.

As a leader, you face the challenge of dealing with this predictable but irrational behaviour of your people. This brings us into the domain of extrinsic and intrinsic motivation, with self-motivation being by far the most interesting option. So ask yourself continuously: is your 'why' worth it? If the effort of your 'why' is higher than the return, you need to think again. Sacrificing ten armies in *Risk* to capture New Zealand, simply because you think it is a fun country, is not a great strategy. But if sacrificing ten armies gives you the whole of Oceania, pin a medal on your chest!

Rebel Talent

We expect artists to be rebellious, but in an organisation rebels are seldom welcome. In her book *Rebel Talent*, the Italian Harvard professor Francesca Gino has written about the value of rebels, both in organisations and in society at large. It is the rebels who search for highly individual solutions, which can perhaps also be useful for everyone. It is also the rebels who can inspire major change through their outrageous creativity. Gino cites the example of Massimo Bottura, now famed as one of the world's top chefs, who was pilloried for many years in his native country, because he dared to tamper with classic Italian recipes.

Francesca Gino, Del Rey Street Books, 2018

WHY YOU OR WHY NOT YOU?

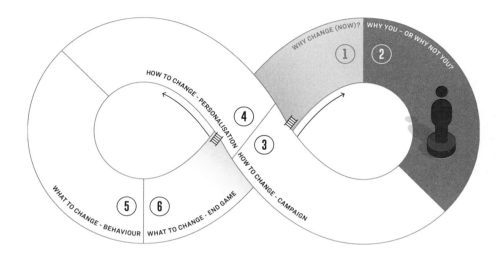

- Why are you the right person to lead this change?
- Do you have experience of similar situations?
- What will this change change for you, your status and your career?
- Is there a crisis and are you sufficiently directive to find your way through it?
- Is the problem 'wicked' and are you an inspirational leader?
- Does the right 'political' climate exist to allow you to be successful?

YOU KNOW WHY YOU WANT TO CHANGE OR MUST CHANGE. The temptation now is to want to take things too quickly. Think back to all the times you have played *Monopoly* – and all the mistakes you have made! Who generally makes the best start in the game? The player who buys every square he lands on? Or the player who buys properties selectively? It's hard to say, since it is largely a question of style and preference. And of luck: throwing six after six gets you around the board quickly and allows you to collect more money from the bank, but it can also make it difficult to buy the properties you want. Even if you do land on a property square, it isn't always easy to make a decision. Say you land on Leicester Square or Atlantic Avenue. Should you buy this reasonably priced, middle-income property or should you wait for the more expensive and more lucrative Mayfair or Boardwalk? And what if you don't then land on Mayfair or Boardwalk? Change processes also force you to look at yourself in this way. Are you the best leader to push through this change? Even if you are the undisputed number one in a small organisation, this is still a question that you need to ask. And even more important is knowing why you are the right person to lead the change – or not.

Change is something you need to learn
—

The status quo is something that leaders find difficult or even threatening. Imagine that as a leader you take over the running of an organisation or department, and that you seemingly do nothing. You just keep everything the way it was. On the face of it, that is fine. You do just as well as your predecessor, even though you perhaps have less experience. The organisation continues to run in the manner with which the stakeholders are familiar. Generating confidence and maintaining tradition in this way is good. However, it might be the case – and usually is – that you feel a certain (often unspoken) pressure from others to do something new. You have just taken over the job, so what added value are you going to bring to it? Perhaps you even ask this question of yourself. Again, that is good, because it may prompt you as the newly appointed leader to put something of yourself into your new role.

This wish brings you automatically to management instruments. 'What can I add?' you ask. 'How can I make a difference?' Your answer? 'Well, we can try to do everything better.' An obvious choice, perhaps, but one that is like music to the ears of your shareholders, employees and customers. Nobody can be against doing things better. But what does it mean, exactly? Working faster? Working cheaper? Being more customer-friendly? Allowing greater creativity? These are the kinds of questions that make the status quo so scary for a new leader. Because they imply a further and more existential question: 'As a leader, do I have a reason for my existence if I change nothing?' And the greater the size of the management team, the greater the urge and the need to make your mark, because the appointment of every new boss is a clear signal that change is on the way. Faced with this situation, you honestly need to ask yourself whether you are planning to implement change for improvement or simply change for change's sake. This is a very difficult balancing act: if you change nothing, you are a charlatan; if you change too much, you don't know what you are doing. To complicate matters still further, you also need to deal with two opposing dynamics: the dynamic in which a leader pushes through change for himself and his own self-image and the dynamic which says that it is okay not to change things. This latter dynamic is often not given the explicit attention it deserves in our modern business culture. An excellent book on this subject and on what makes an ideal leader is *Why Should Anyone Be Led By You* by Robert Goffee and Gareth Jones.

" Ask yourself whether you are planning to implement change for improvement or simply change for change's sake.

In addition to the pressure on a new leader to change, account also needs to be taken of the binary perspective on changing and not changing. There is frequently a tendency to think that change needs to be immediately far-reaching; otherwise, it will not be thorough and effective. This approach does not work. Change is something that you need to learn. Unfortunately, learning how to manage change is a much-neglected subject, both in society in general – look at the political world with its compulsion to act and the difficulties we are experiencing in dealing effectively with climate change because of people's reluctance to change their lifestyle, even though mankind has never been faced with a more urgent burning platform – and in the business world in particular. Imagine, however, that a new leader decides to look closely at all aspects of the organisation, but then concludes that nothing needs to be changed. In its own way, that is also a change process. It is simply that its impact is less obvious.

If an organisation has learnt how to manage change properly, subsequent change trajectories will be less painful. The idea of change will have permeated the entire organisational structure and everyone knows that things will never be changed just for the sake of it. This results in a healthy organisation with a high changeability factor. Such organisations are able to respond quickly to the internal and external 'whys', no matter how or when they appear. Often, minor changes are taking place all the time, but they are not experienced as being drastic or dramatic, because people know that if something is working well, not changing it will always be an acceptable option. Learning when to change and when not to change is all part of this learning process. To remain healthy, organisations need to ensure that there is transparency and intense communication on all matters relating to change. Companies with production processes are a good example, in both a positive and a negative sense. For example, in one company it may be standard practice at the end of each shift for the outgoing team to inform the incoming team about things that worked well and things that caused problems, so that the new team can react accordingly. In another company, the outgoing shift supervisor might simply pass the necessary keys to his incoming colleague, with no other hand-over of any kind. If he fails to mention that just for today one of the machines has been set to work more slowly for this or that reason, a crucial learning moment will be lost, so that the machine might continue to run at the wrong setting for days or even weeks.

An interesting distinction within this learning process is the distinction between life-critical and non-life-critical situations. In my job, the decisions I take can affect people's lives, but are seldom (if ever) life-threatening or life-saving. This situation is very different for someone who works for the fire service. Delaying some decisions for as little as 30 seconds might potentially cost someone his or her life. For this reason, after every intervention fire-fighting teams undergo an extensive debriefing: what was perfect, what was good, what was less good, what was bad, etc? In many instances, these sessions are recorded, so that they can be useful for other teams. Similar procedures are also used in hospitals and in military units. This kind of After Action Review (AAR) is essential not so much to learn from mistakes, since these will always be investigated fully, but primarily to identify and learn from near-mistakes, which might otherwise slip under the radar. For an AAR to be effective, it is necessary for the hierarchy to be temporarily put to one side, because it is crucial during such sessions that people feel able to speak freely about everything. It is an example that organisations in many other sectors would do well to follow.

THE OPERATION WAS SUCCESSFUL, BUT THE PATIENT IS DEAD!

The concept of the After Action Review, a thorough process of debriefing, originated in the armed forces. It is now also used by the emergency services and has also become standard practice in many hospitals. And with beneficial results. In the United States, researchers investigated why some surgical procedures were significantly more successful in some hospitals than in others. They discovered that a number of factors were involved, ranging from the interaction between the surgeon and the nursing staff to the level of hygiene in the operating theatre. But the most decisive factor of all was the discussability of mistakes and near-mistakes. Fewer lessons were learnt in hospitals with a strict hierarchy, because this made it near-impossible to criticise or question the surgical team. But if a nurse can never contradict the opinion of a surgeon, it becomes impossible for either of them to ever do their job properly. The need for everyone to be recognised in their job is essential for creating a healthy dynamic. In hospitals where the hierarchy was disregarded during the AAR, the learning process was much stronger.

The founder is dead, long live the founder!
—

The extent to which an organisation learns from its mistakes and is willing to change is strongly linked to the nature of the organisational culture. In some organisations, there is a reflex to find a scapegoat when mistakes are made. Sometimes, things are taken even a stage further: 'It was that employee's fault, and so we have dismissed that employee, because it was a capital error, and now the problem is solved!' Of course, nothing has been solved. The dismissed employee will probably have had an impact on the situation, but the underlying cause of the mistake will not disappear simply because the employee in question has been removed. This line of reasoning is equivalent to saying that the best way to make no mistakes is to do nothing, or to blame someone else when something goes wrong. You would not believe in how many organisations that is still the case. The only way to change this mentality is to change the organisational culture. And to achieve this, you first have to know how a culture develops and can be directed. This – for me, at least – is a fascinating subject, but one that seems scarcely to occupy the thoughts of most CEOs and boards of directors.

❞ To change an organisational culture, you need to return to the roots of that culture.

To change an organisational culture, you need to return to the roots of that culture. In this context, one essential question that consultants often forget to ask is this: 'Is the founder still alive?' I mean this both literally and figuratively. In most organisations, and particularly in small and medium-sized ones, the influence of the founder(s) on the organisational culture is both massive and lasting. If the founder is still alive and still active in the company, this influence is exercised on a daily basis. But even if they are dead and buried, founders continue to have an influence, albeit at a different and more intangible level. Legendary stories are told about them, stories that often surpass reality. Such is the nature of tradition! Urban myths develop that are only loosely connected with the truth, becoming more and more fabulous each time they are told. Like the story of the gigantic alligators that are supposed to be swimming through the sewers of New York. There are none, of course, but this does not stop people believing in them, and they get bigger with each new telling.

In an organisation, stories of this kind influence what is possible and not possible. For example, there is a large Belgian media company that still holds moments of reflection for its staff in the company chapel on the eve of religious festivals, even though the Catholic founder has been dead for many years and most of the employees are non-believers. And if the founder is still alive, the situation becomes even more complex. The only way to change a culture in these circumstances is to first get the founder to support the change. Cultural change works top-down. Trying to make it work bottom-up is a complete non-starter. The founder always injects his or her personality into the organisation. This means that if there are certain things that he or she finds important, there is a very good chance that these things will find expression within the organisational culture. Things that the founder considers to be less important will receive less attention. Creating sufficient bottom-up weight to counter-balance this situation is only possible if there is extreme openness within the organisation. Because even in organisations where there is a high degree of employee participation and where new ideas are given the opportunity to flourish, in the final analysis it is still the founder who decides just how far such participation and ideas will be allowed to go. The same applies to ideas from outside the organisation: it is the founder who decides what influence they will be allowed to have.

In this context, it is interesting to consider the position of family-run companies. These are often subject to a dual influence: the continuing influence of the founder and the new influence of his/her successor. There is a possibility that the personalities of these two leaders will be similar, but they will always have different views on certain matters, if for no other reason than the generation gap. A leader who grew up during the last quarter of the previous century or the first decades of the current century will be more likely to see the need for digitalisation than a leader who grew up in the period 1945 to 1975. To change an organisational culture based on these foundations, you need to have a conscious awareness of who you are and what you want. Just like people who consciously work at their own self-development regularly ask themselves how they wish to behave towards others and what they wish to stand for in their life, so you, as a leader or a founder, need to think consciously about how you want to behave as a person, about how you want the organisation to behave and what you want it to represent to the outside world, about what practices are acceptable or unacceptable, and so on. The answers to these questions will determine your culture. Consider, for example, the question of how to deal with ageing employees. Do you think that older employees are less efficient and should therefore be jettisoned or do you think that their experience allows them to continue making a valued contribution, so that they should be treated with respect? Likewise, how do you respond to mistakes? Are they something you can learn from or are they something to be covered up at all costs? As soon as there are two authority figures in an organisation, you will have potentially divergent views on matters of this kind. And if something happens, it is often the case that one will conceal his or her views from the other, in an attempt to avoid tension and defuse the situation. These human dynamics and processes are fascinating and they also have a major influence on organisational culture.

Complicated? Then imagine that instead of just two people being involved, there are a thousand. Or ten thousand. This generates not only many more dynamics, but also many more stories and symbols. Some symbols can be seemingly innocuous, like the photograph of the founder in the entrance hall of the company's premises, but such symbols are also associated with stories; powerful anecdotes that have an influence on the company culture. These are symbols that say: 'This is how we got to where we are today and that is the way we should stay'. The impact of symbols and history is often seriously underestimated, frequently because CEOs fail to deal with them consciously. At the same time, the distance between a culture and a cult can sometimes be very small. The Colruyt family, founder and owner of one of the largest supermarket chains in Belgium, has developed a cult status. The family devotes huge attention to personal development. One of the sisters has a centre in a delightful setting, where many of the Colruyt training courses focused on self-realisation are given. The same thrust is also strongly embedded in the way the company does things, including its treatment of its employees. But the family symbols, inherited from the grandfather who first founded the company, as well as the many stories dating from those pioneering days, are still very much a part of Colruyt's organisational persona. In this way, the Colruyt family tree, the Colruyt way of thinking and the experience of the Colruyt company are all seamlessly interwoven.

One of the most fascinating examples that I ever saw of this symbiosis perfectly illustrates the light and dark side of human nature. Jef Colruyt, the current paterfamilias, drew a simple mountain, which represented a person. Like a mountain, people's strengths allow them to rise above the low-lying plains. And as those strengths grow, so the mountain gets bigger and bigger. Colruyt next drew a sun on one side of the mountain and said: 'The bigger the mountain, the bigger its shadow side'. This is a wonderful image, full of spiritual insight. It also says much about the way that Colruyt deals with people. It accepts that while everyone has a sunny side, they also have a darker side; that while they have strengths, they also have weaknesses. Colruyt uses a simple common language that connects all its people. But by working in this manner, Colruyt also creates a cult – and not everyone feels comfortable with that. The question that founders and leaders need to ask themselves is therefore this: do you consciously wish to go further than the creation of a culture, so that you end up creating a cult?

Merging is losing
—

One of the most difficult change trajectories or transformation processes is the merger of two or more companies, or the integration of one organisation into another. The main reason why mergers and integrations seldom create the expected added value is that the differences in the cultures involved generate clashes that reduce efficiency. It is like wanting to play *The Settlers of Catan* with the rules of *Carcassonne*! Part of the problem is that reconciling differing cultures is one of the aspects of mergers that generally receives little attention. The matching of the information systems, the harmonising of salary scales, the rationalisation of processes: these matters are all given careful consideration, but nine times out of ten the question of whether the employees of the merged entities can relate to each other in the same manner is overlooked.

There is one issue with mergers that causes more problems than all the rest: is it a merger of equals? A merger of equals means that one party does not dominate the other. This in turn means that you need to shape a new joint culture together, with both partners having the same amount of input. The new culture is therefore the result of the mutual agreements that are made. You can compare it with a blended family. Here, too, there is (hopefully!) a need for an amalgamation of equals. If one of the partners has children or they both have children and are planning to live in a new house, there are a hundred and one things that need to be arranged (as far as possible) to everyone's satisfaction. This newly composed family can either resurrect old rules or make completely new ones; for example, about breakfasting together, use of the bathroom, screen time for the kids, and so on. This is a tiring process, but has an objective that makes the effort worthwhile: together, we are going to create something new. However, this process is much more difficult if one of the partners is over-dominant. If one of the partners with children moves into the house of the other partner and simply accepts his or her existing house rules, that is a very clear choice but it is no longer possible to speak of a new joint culture. In the business world, there is not even a choice involved in such situations: the subservient partner has no option but to follow the wishes of the dominant partner, like it or not.

An additional difficulty is the fact that the companies involved in the merger have often been each other's competitors for many years. And because they have been competitors, they both have stories about why they are better than their erstwhile rival and why they would never want to work with them. Over the years, these feelings have also been incorporated into their symbols and people need symbols. If you bring together two groups of people and if you give them a blue and a red shirt, it will not be long before the blue team develops a blue identity and the red team develops a red identity, with both teams regarding themselves as better than the other. And then you suddenly expect them to join forces and play in the same team? Hardly realistic, is it? A good example of the impracticality of this thinking can be found in the Belgian media world. For many years, the outspoken *Humo* magazine poked fun at the more popular *Dag Allemaal*, until the day when both titles were merged into the DPG Media group. Suddenly, the *Humo* editors who had looked down their noses at their *Dag Allemaal* colleagues now discovered that they were forced to rub shoulders with each other in the hip coffee bar of their brand-new company premises!

A very different example relates to the ice-cream manufacturer Ben & Jerry's, which for political and humanitarian reasons decided to no longer sell its blue pots of happiness in occupied Palestinian territory. This was a decision that infuriated the Israeli government, which made its anger known to Unilever, the mother company of Ben & Jerry's. Unilever answered that it still regarded Israel as one of its trading partners, but nevertheless at the same time wished to give freedom of decision-making to its Ben & Jerry's subsidiary. In other words, two entities within the same organisation were steering a diametrically opposite course. So how do you deal with a situation like that? How can you direct such a process? In these circumstances, the human and more emotional side of a merger or takeover seldom gets the necessary guidance it needs.

" **When a merger is taking place, make the rules of the game clear from the start and communicate those rules transparently. And make sure you communicate them to everyone involved, since this is the best way to get as many people on board with the least possible delay.**

Once again, we arrive back at the 'why'. Why merge? Why opt to impose a particular culture as dominant? Imagine that one company in a holding has a reputation for extravagance and another company in the same holding has a reputation for thrift. You could easily argue that the best solution in this situation is to merge the two companies and impose the culture of the latter on the former. Such a decision would no doubt be taken with the best of intentions.

CHANGE CAN BE CHILD'S PLAY

But let us further imagine that the first company has a warm culture that stimulates creativity (albeit with a high level of expenditure), whereas the second company has a colder and more business-like approach. This would result in the culture of the first company being smothered, so that we would no longer be talking about a merger but about an aggressive takeover.

When a merger is taking place, make the rules of the game clear from the start and communicate those rules transparently. And make sure you communicate them to everyone involved, since this is the best way to get as many people on board with the least possible delay. The unions obviously play a key role in this and it important to align the conditions on which they can agree. Take the best from one side, the best from the other side, and then negotiate your way towards the middle. It is only to be expected that this will have cost implications, and in practice this cost is generally higher than the expectation, because the financial conditions of the merging parties need to be levelled up, since levelling down in neither desirable nor legal. Procedures also need to be aligned, because it is annoying if, for example, two colleagues need to apply for their annual leave in different ways. This explains why after a merger it is better to create a single joint culture. But not aggressively. The easiest option is to choose a culture and then work towards assimilation. But remember that people do not like to be assimilated...

Measuring and credibility
—

In the business world, data is the new gold of the 21st century. Data is useful in many different ways. As a result, data mining is very much 'in'. Data are a fantastic measuring instrument for organisations, because it allows them to 'prove' that they are doing well. Without data to back it up, this claim is just so much hot air. You can play *belote* all afternoon, but if no one is keeping the score you will never know who has won and who has lost. Perhaps it has something to do with my sporting background and my ambition to be the best squash player in the world, but I am a big fan of rankings. True, ranking systems are not always perfect and the point scores are not always as accurate as they could be, but at least it makes it possible for you to say quickly and easily whether or not, according to the ranking, you are number one. What's more, a permanent ranking system makes it possible to make quick adjustments. Which meaningful measurements can you use to check regularly whether or not you are moving in the right direction? And by this I mean elements other than cost and profit, since these inspire and motivate only a very few people.

We have already seen that emergency services such as the fire brigade make use of a highly interesting learning process. These services analyse their interventions, so that they can save even more lives or prevent more damage. These are different measurement criteria from the business world, where the focus is on efficiency and the aforementioned cost and profit. If these latter elements become a goal in themselves, they inevitably result in a perverse organisational culture. If, as an organisation, you are only concerned about making money, your people will soon start thinking about how they can make more money than their colleagues. In other words, colleagues become competitors, which can only be useful for a limited number of business activities. Of course, this does not mean that attempting to make a profit is in any way 'dishonourable'. In the economy-conscious and commercialised world in which we live, making a healthy profit is a self-evident necessity. However, the choice of words here is important. What is healthy? You can only know this if you first answer another question: why do you really do what you do?

Another 'why' that you need to deal with carefully is sustainability. Every business leader knows that sustainability has a clear appeal and at the very least needs to be included somewhere in a slogan. Remember, however, that most people have a built-in detector that effectively recognises bullshit. A producer of biological wine, who has made his entire production chain from grape to bottle as environmentally friendly as he can, is someone who works sustainably. A manufacturer of PVC windows also works sustainably, since plastic lasts for ever and requires no replacement. In other words, they can both stick the label 'sustainable' on their products and would both be justified in doing so, but in most people's eyes there will clearly be a difference in perception. In addition, there is also the question of personal credibility. A business leader who is always talking about sustainability but has an exuberant lifestyle will come across as much less credible than a business leader who donates part of his wealth to good causes. Once again, this is a question of perception rather than a value judgement, since both leaders are capable of living a lifestyle that would put most of us in the shade. But the message is clear: if you wish to play the sustainability card as your 'why', you need to move beyond trite slogans. 'Wanting to create a better world' is an obviously usable 'why' for an organisation like Greenpeace, but less so for a bank. So how can you translate that intention for a bank? You can take as your starting point the idea that a bank is an important part of the economic fabric. This is a rational position, but hardly an inspiring one. Consequently, you need to take things further: a bank is an important part of the economic fabric, which helps the economy to flourish, stimulates entrepreneurship and allows people to improve the quality of their life and to realise their dreams. This is a more inspirational formulation and allows you to make the link to 'wanting to create a better world'. In this way, you fill in your 'why' in a credible manner, with sustainability as a valid part of the equation. The difficulty lies in keeping the 'how' and the 'what' equally credible. In short: you have to practice what you preach.

When it comes to sustainability, an organisation's vehicle fleet is an easy target for critics. At the same time, it is a difficult criticism for companies to tackle, because in many countries it is cheaper for employers to give their employees a company car and a petrol card than to pay the equivalent in wages. As a result, there are still a huge number of company cars on our roads – and cars and sustainability are not an easy tandem to combine. Consequently, there is societal pressure to change. Scrapping company cars is good news for the tax authorities (whose revenue would increase), but bad news for the employers (whose costs would also increase). Perhaps the solution can be found by looking at the sustainable aspects of the vehicles that make up the vehicle fleet? For example, the 'i-mens' home nursing service recently decided to replace its entire fleet of 1,200 vehicles with more sustainable hybrid models, which are also available after working hours for members of the Cambio car-sharing scheme.

This is a clever example of credible sustainability, which won both praise and prizes for the organisation concerned. But the story needs to be consistent and authentic. If, as a company, you opt for a sustainable vehicle fleet, while the CEO is still driving around in a petrol-guzzling Porche, no one will believe your story and your 'why' will lose its authenticity. In this case, sustainability is just a slogan, not a way of life. Again, this is not a judgement and it is not my intention to divide people up into 'good' and 'bad'. These are simply choices that people make. If you opt for sustainability, you must also have the courage to look at the trade-offs that you are prepared to make. If you say that sustainability is important to you, it is crucial that this not only finds expression in your 'why', 'how' and 'what', but also that it is consistently applied. *Bluff It* is a fun game for all the family, but one that requires you to play fast and loose with credibility. Real credibility implies both saying and doing. It frequently happens that an organisation's story is not always consistent, particularly with larger companies, where it is often a question of saying one thing and doing another. A typical example in recent years is the idea of increasing internal collaboration within the organisation by making everyone work in open-plan offices. As a result, people find themselves sitting without a fixed desk in vast open spaces, where there may indeed be more contact and better co-operation with colleagues, but also more complaints about too much noise and the difficulty to concentrate properly. However, this is to be expected: few changes only have benefits. No, that is not the problem. The real problem is that up on the senior management floor the directors and heads of department are still sitting in their own spacious offices, complete with a separate room for their secretaries and facilities for welcoming visitors! Not really consistent, would you say?

Another example? In the last decade or so, many companies have switched to the paperless office. This is now feasible: traditional letters have largely been replaced by e-mails and colleagues can often work at the same time on the same document via the use of an internal server or the cloud. Even so, I still know of a number of companies where an administrative clerk prints off all the e-mails and places them on the desk of the CEO. Again, this hardly suggests a genuinely consistent story. At the same time, it also illustrates how much the perception of the CEO's role has changed in recent times. In the past, if you wanted to reach the CEO as a customer, supplier or partner, you sent a letter that was almost certainly not opened by the CEO in person. Because a CEO who opened all his own mail was probably not a good CEO. In fact, there was a strong likelihood that the CEO would never get to see your letter, because there were at least two filters between the company letter box and his office, where more junior officials would decide whether or not it was a subject that he needed to be bothered about. The things that eventually did arrive on the CEO's desk had therefore been pre-selected twice. This had two main consequences: the CEO did not need to waste time on matters that were not directly his concern, but it also meant that he was not fully aware of the questions, complaints and other issues that were concerning the company's customers, suppliers and partners. Today, we expect that CEOs will deal with all their own e-mails, which essentially requires them to carry out a simple administrative function: the filtering of incoming digital correspondence. This clearly leads to a loss of efficiency, but at the same time it also offers a potential gain in terms of sustainability. The ambition of promoting greater internal sustainability also implies a preference for a particular way of working. Why do you really want to do this? Is it based on a desire to reduce your company's carbon footprint? Or is it perhaps linked to a sense of responsibility to leave the world in a better state than you found it? There are, of course, numerous potential drivers, which all come back to the kind of leader you want to be.

The visible versus the invisible leader
—

I have already mentioned how a company culture sometimes tips over into a cult. Such a cult is always person-related and sometimes its creation is necessary as a kind of useful provocation, because a cult is always more provocative than a culture. The cult stands or falls with the founder, or at the very least on the visibility of the CEO. This visibility can be internal, external or both.

For example, Wouter Torfs of the Belgian shoe store chain of the same name is a highly visible CEO, both internally and externally. Externally, he features regularly in the company's advertising, offers his opinions on a range of subjects in the press, and organises eye-catching promotional stunts, such as giving away thousands of pairs of shoes following the 2021 floods. Is this philanthropy or is it just clever PR? Who can say – but it is certainly visible. Internally, Torfs also has the same high level of visibility and his philosophy of life is firmly embedded in every branch of the company. As a result, Torfs has repeatedly been chosen as the best employer in the country, even though 90 percent of his store staff have probably never met him.

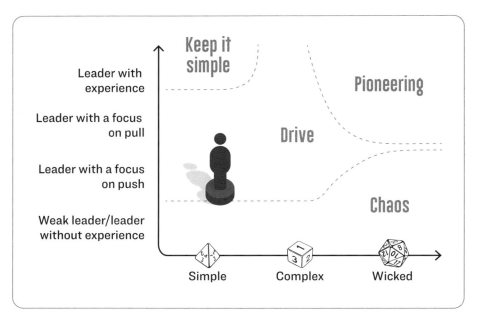

The influence of leadership style on the change process

This personal visibility gives the organisational culture a face. This is vital, because an organisation without a face is like a campaign without a standard bearer. The disadvantage is, of course, that the standard bearer always becomes idealised – and that is the way he or she remains. As a fifth-generation company leader, you may find yourself struggling to compete with the memory of a sacrosanct predecessor, who everyone still reveres, even though he has long been dead. In this situation, it is the new CEO's difficult but necessary task to try and strike the right balance between the achievements of the past and what the organisation needs today. How are you going to integrate modern technologies and methods into old values and usages? Imagine that your company has been making gas stoves for several decades. The possibilities open to you are much more limited than those enjoyed by the founder all those years ago. Especially if the prediction that gas supplies will have run out by 2050 is accurate. So what can you do? You need to think carefully about what good things you can carry over from the past that will help you to successfully deal with changing circumstances in the future.

On the other side of the coin, there is also such a thing as the invisible CEO. There can be various reasons for this invisibility: the nature of the sector, the nature of the organisation, the nature of the product or service, and so on. Less visibility can also be a conscious choice, because the CEO feels better that way or because he/she regards a high personal profile as unimportant. Even so, this is something that the CEOs in question need to think about very carefully. Why? Because this choice determines whether or not you will have a lever to make use of your culture, consciously or unconsciously. At the same time, it also determines the extent to which you will be able (or not able) to make use of certain key instruments. For example, a leader who prefers to remain behind the scenes will not be able to take part in a creative advertising campaign based on his or her person. Everyone in Belgium (or at least in Flanders) knows Donald Muylle, the founder of Dovy Kitchens. Dovy's TV advertisements, famed for his bad acting and his bumbling approach, have become legendary. As a result, Dovy has a high level of brand recognisability and their slogans even appear occasionally in other walks of life. In contrast, Philippe Taminiaux, the founder of Eggo Kitchens, is much less visible to the general public, so that the company's advertising seems less warm and less personal.

> **Internal visibility can also be useful for putting extra weight behind the change process or, in some cases, for even kick-starting that process into life.**

One of these approaches is not necessarily better or worse than the other. But it is something that CEOs need to reflect on at length. Because a CEO who at first wishes to remain in the background but then later decides to move into the spotlight can create a counterproductive effect. It is like when you are playing *Monopoly*: there are different kinds of players. Some accumulate money quietly, others shriek with delight when someone lands on one of their hotels, boasting of how rich this makes them. If you are the first kind of player, but subsequently try to change into the second kind, this will not increase your chances of winning the game. Quite the reverse: because you will not feel comfortable with your new persona, this may lead you to make more mistakes.

Internal visibility can also be useful for putting extra weight behind the change process or, in some cases, for even kick-starting that process into life. Imagine that you are the new leader in a company where a cult already exists and where the same practices have held sway for years. These might be practices that first originated when social norms were very different; for example, in the field of health and safety. Over the years, the company has become very careless in these matters, but without any serious consequences – so far. They remain within the letter of the law, but only just. As the new leader, this is an area where you do not wish to accept anything that can compromise the safety of your people. However, this effectively changes it into a personal issue, because it means that you will need to go against tradition. To have any chance of success, you will need high internal visibility, since this is the only way to give a face to the change you desire. This is even more imperative if you want to push through changes that are not strictly speaking necessary or are even seen as wholly unnecessary. This will mean confrontation, and you need to be very sure of why you are doing what you are doing. Is the change necessary for the shareholders? For your career? For the sustainability of the organisation? For the employees? The best changes are the ones for which you can tick off all these boxes. Moreover, a change that offers benefits for everyone is also the easiest kind of change to push through. In fact, there is no need to convince anyone; people simply jump on board. But it is not always like that: 'Dear shareholder, we are going to do something that will significantly improve staff safety, but it will mean a reduced dividend this year...' That is a message that is much less easy to sell. You will then need to argue that sailing close to the wind with healthy and safety regulations is a risky practice that needs to stop before someone gets badly hurt. Perhaps you can wait until an official safety check shows that there is a serious problem and sets a deadline for putting it right? Not such a good idea, because this brings you back to the status quo. As long as nothing happened, your predecessors kept quiet about the risks and just carried on as normal. Are you now going to do the same? Or do you simply not want the problem to become official on your watch? This runs contrary to the urge to perform and the fear of the status quo that is common to most CEOs. So think again.

The extent to which a CEO can bring about change in an organisation is dependent to a significant degree on personal motivation and ambition. Making a career – in other words, having ambition – is important. Otherwise, you would never have made it to CEO in the first place. Another important factor is the limited 'sell-by date' of most CEOs. In the United States, this is now expressed in terms of months, rather than years. In the world's top 500 companies, the CEO stays on average for something less than 24 months. And if you know that you do not have much time, the urgency to prove yourself quickly becomes that much greater. But how exactly? Do you take on existing projects that have been put on the back-burner, waiting for the right moment? Or do you generate new initiatives? Alternatively, you can try to search for the right momentum that will allow your people to set the agenda for you. This will largely be a matter of chance. If, for example, you see that a particular team in the organisation makes fewer mistakes and has less sickness absence than all the others, it is often a good idea to take a look at what things that team is doing differently. Using this knowledge, you can then start a change trajectory for all the other teams.

Consciously experimenting is also an option. For example, you can investigate what you can learn from how the local fire service conducts its consultations, briefings and debriefings. Or you can ask if their learning process has been documented and disseminated, not only to various teams but also to various different regions, so that these regions can consult with each other, in a manner that might allow your own teams and regions to adopt something similar. This is something that poses a challenge in almost every organisation, because it is astonishing how differently different teams function from each other and even communicate with each other. A good example of this was cited in the book *Team of Teams*, in which the American general Stanley A. McChrystal told how the US military, as part of its fight against Al Qaeda in Iraq, wanted to put together a composite team consisting of top units from the army, navy, air force, intelligence, and so on. The idea was to give this small group of elite servicemen and women the opportunity to experiment and then share what they had learnt with the entire military network. However, it soon became clear that all these different units spoke a different kind of language, had a different way of debriefing their personnel, and had different approaches to hierarchy and the distribution of authority! The plan was eventually shelved, proving that in situations of this kind the first thing that you need to do is find a common language. But the basic idea of a small, experimental group gathering and then sharing their knowledge remains sound and can be useful in any organisation.

Not every change is a change

The most obvious change processes are pushed by external factors. For instance, new legislation or changes in the operational context always have a compelling effect. But this does not mean that the change process is carefully planned and well thought through. In recent times, we have all experienced a classic example of this: the corona pandemic. This crisis had a massive impact on our way of working and even on our way of living. Whether that impact was temporary or permanent, and at what levels, remains to be seen. One thing that we can say for certain is that COVID-19 was a massive accelerant, especially in the field of digitalisation. But is it really possible to speak of a change process? Many companies boasted with pride about how in the course of a single weekend they were able to switch over to digital working. But if you look at this claim in detail, it usually relates to the use of specific instruments, such as Zoom or Microsoft Teams. So, technically speaking, the boast was correct: there was a switchover. But were those instruments used effectively? If you ever took part in a Zoom meeting, you will probably have experienced that most of the time half of the participants' cameras were not in active mode, perhaps because the bandwidth was inadequate, or because it is tiring to follow multiple screens simultaneously, or because they just got bored... In other words, you miss the essence of what is happening. It is a bit like turning on the television to listen to the radio. At the start of the lockdown, Zoom was fun, because you saw everyone's facial expression, could laugh with each other, and so on. Now, Zoom has more or less been reduced to the status of a glorified telephone call – which means that the instrument is not being used correctly.

With Microsoft Teams this is even more the case. Teams is an instrument for speaking to each other online, but also a platform on which documents can be shared in a highly transparent manner. As a result, each team member has immediate sight of the latest version of the document and a number of them can all work on the document at the same time, within the limits of a group that you are able to define. Teams therefore offers numerous possibilities for working in a different way. Even so, during the past two years the vast majority of organisations have changed very little about the way they work. All that has changed is the way they hold meetings. These meetings are now held online, but then everyone goes their separate ways to work on their own documents. Once again, the instrument is not being used properly.

" Put simply, the corona crisis has changed things superficially, but there is still a long way to go before we can talk about a new way of working. If we want to achieve this, we need to go back to the 'why'. During the pandemic, the 'why' was formulated on the basis of crisis thinking.

Put simply, the corona crisis has changed things superficially, but there is still a long way to go before we can talk about a new way of working. If we want to achieve this, we need to go back to the 'why'. During the pandemic, the 'why' was formulated on the basis of crisis thinking. The reasoning was: 'We can no longer work with each other physically. So how can we solve this problem? Let's work at distance. How? What are we going to do? Let's give everyone a laptop, so that they can meet and work online from home!' That is how things went in the majority of companies, but it was a missed opportunity to make more efficient and more comfortable working over the long term their real 'why'. However, that would have required more effort and more resources to work out the 'how' and the 'what'. Take working from home, for example. During the first months of the pandemic there was a positive feeling, because it was great to be able to work in your own house all day: no more traffic jams, no more need to avoid your irritating colleagues, freedom to take a break whenever you want, and so on. But after a time it became clear that the kitchen table, or the spare room, or the cellar, or wherever else you tried to find a bit of peace and quiet, so that you could concentrate, was not the ideal working location. You could put up with it for a while, because it was a crisis situation, but it was not a sustainable long-term solution.

Now that the world has got back to normal (more or less), I am receiving an increasing number of requests from companies about their 'how'. It has become fashionable for many organisations to say that they do not want to return to 'the way things used to be'. I agree with them entirely, but which instruments are they willing to use to make this possible? For example, some boards of directors are now discussing whether to give their staff the right to work from home two or three days per week. Others approach the problem from the other side and say that no one will have the right to work 100 percent from home, whilst allowing the employees a degree of latitude to fix the percentage. These are both legitimate positions to take, but in both cases you will need an instrument that can effectively monitor the new working arrangements. Once again, you need to ask: what is your 'why'? Is it to cut costs? That is certainly one possible reason: before the corona crisis broke out, many companies had plans to build new and larger premises, which have now been scaled back because in the future only half the personnel will be in the office at any one time. Or is it to strengthen collaboration? Or to improve the quality of life for your people? These are all valid reasons, but make sure that you do not underestimate their impact on the organisation.

Imagine that two people in the same team are both allowed to work from home for three days each week. This might mean that they never actually see each other! Depending on the nature of their work, that might not be a major problem, but at the very least it creates a distance between them. Team members who never see each other will no longer feel like colleagues and, consequently, will no longer behave like colleagues. Team members who do see each other, even if only occasionally and particularly in pleasurable contexts, are able to build up a connection. At the same time, new arrangements of this kind also increase the distance between the employee and the organisation as a whole, which perhaps makes them more open to offers to go and work elsewhere. Again, you need to find new instruments to monitor and steer this new situation. Have you ever tried to run a team whose members are seldom or never able to meet as an entire group? Believe me, it is not easy. To start with, you need to make a disciplined analysis of the elements of the work for which some people will inevitably need to meet physically, if efficiency is to be maintained. Broader meetings? These do not need to be physical, but can take place online, providing the technology is used correctly. Brainstorming is more difficult, because physical proximity often stimulates the creative process. Above all – and this is something many organisations overlook – successes need to be celebrated together, and not at a distance. Some companies tried this distance approach during the corona crisis, even to the extent of sending packets of celebratory food and drink to the people who were working at home. This was all done with the best of intentions and in a crisis situation many have helped to boost team spirit to some degree, but it will certainly not work over the long term.

The problem with changes that are pushed through quickly, as was so often the case in the wake of the corona crisis, is that all too often organisations attempt to apply general rules. They use a passe-partout, into which they wish to slot each and every employee. For instance, agreeing that everyone can work two days a week from home. No alternative. No flexibility. Of course, it doesn't work. To begin with, you need to take account of the nature of the work involved. You can hardly let the aircrew we mentioned earlier in the book work from home! The same applies to our two warehouse storemen. Okay, perhaps in theory they could become home workers with a joystick and a good online connection, but in that case you could just as easily employ a robot. Perhaps these are silly examples, but you get the point. The need for efficiency ensures that the general rule is weakened to become a general rule that applies to everyone, except in situations where working from home is impossible. Which means that it is no longer a general rule…

But even in sectors where working from home is theoretically possible, there will still need to be diversity. It is not possible for everyone to benefit from your general rule. Drivers cannot work at home. Receptionists cannot work at home. Cleaners cannot work at home. The result is that you have a general rule that only applies to part of your personnel. True, you can draw up a list of exceptions, but this is not good for creating cohesion within the organisation.

Why? Because you are dealing with a 'right' that not everyone is able to enjoy. And that is just the first of the major problems! In addition, there is also no proper way of assessing the effectiveness and the other possible positive and negative consequences of the general rule. The corona lockdown in Belgium only led to a relatively small drop in productivity. In administrative functions, there was more or less a status quo. As a result, many organisations have put home working on their permanent agenda. At first glance, this sounds like a measure that primarily benefits the employees, but in general there is also a cost-saving 'why' involved. The company can move to smaller premises, can save on energy and transport costs, and so on. But does it actually improve performance? The honest answer is that we simply do not know. But now that the first euphoria of working at home has passed, it seems likely that it will do little to make people work better, unless there is a significant increase in comfort.

In psychology, research has been carried out involving children who are never touched. The conclusion was that this is an ideal way to create psychopaths. What would be the effect on colleagues if they were no longer able to see each other or share the same working space? It is unlikely that they will become psychopaths, but it would certainly create a distance between them, which is not a helpful dynamic in a working environment. Because doing things together is an important part of what makes work meaningful. Who will you be working with? Will you like them? Can you learn from them? Can you have a laugh with them? Can you go for a beer with them? This is a valuable part of the work experience. I am not arguing against working from home; all I am saying is that you need to think carefully about which instruments you will use. And for implementing change, general rules are a very blunt instrument indeed! These are factors that you need to take into account right from the very start of your change trajectory. Once you have decided on your 'why', choosing the right leader to implement it is crucial. Managers or other leaders who think in terms of general rules or who like to simplify things as much as possible are very useful when it comes to less complex change. But for a complex 'why', and certainly for a wicked 'why', you would be well advised to look for a different kind of leader. If you are more the first kind of leader than the second, you will need to swallow your pride and hand over the change leadership to someone who is better suited.

Landing is more difficult than flying

The three sequences of change – the 'why', the 'how' and the 'what' – can be compared with an aeroplane that is coming in to land. In the first phase, you are flying at 40,000 feet and can hardly see the ground. In the second phase, you descend to 20,000 feet and can see the ground clearly. Here and there, you can even recognise certain details. In the 'what' phase, you descend still further, until you are just one foot from the ground. You are about to land and hopefully all will go well. Why at 40,000 feet during the first phase? Because your 'why' is always abstract. Why do you want to do something? To make the world a better place! A noble idea, but somewhat vague. You therefore need to make the 'how' and the 'what' much more concrete, even if the 'why' itself has a concrete origin. Imagine, for example, that your 'why' is based on a change in the law. This is extremely concrete, but not very inspiring. Okay, maybe some people find it 'inspirational' to play by the rules – but not very many of them.

The 'why' is generally the level within the organisation about which people can agree, although it is often far from clear precisely what they agree about. Because the 'why' is purely indicative. Imagine that the mission of a company is to improve people's quality of life. Everyone in the company, from the lowliest cleaner to the most senior manager, will be able to support that mission. But they will probably all have different opinions about what 'improving

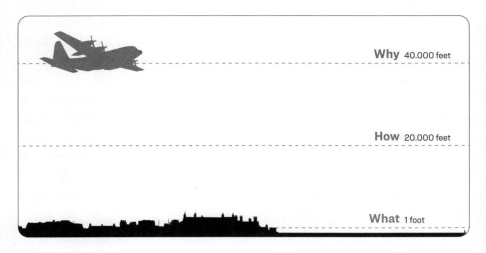

The change process is like a plane coming in to land. In the 'why' phase, everything is abstract. It is only when the plane starts its descent that things become clearer.

people's quality of life' actually means. I might regard a number of things as being important in life, whereas you might find my choices completely irrelevant – and vice versa. For this reason, there is no point in trying to make the 'why' phase more concrete. If your aim is, say, to improve the quality of life for a hundred thousand people, you need to understand that you will never be able to reach and motivate (or even frustrate) all those people in the same manner. Consequently, the 'why' phase can only be an expression of intent. And precisely for that reason, it is an important moment to secure alignment within the organisation's leadership team. We often talk about individual leaders and the concept of leadership, but within organisations the leadership team is just as important and influential. The question that this team needs to answer with unanimity is this: how important is this 'why' in our list of priorities and are we going to completely commit to it together?

At Deloitte, a few years ago, we developed a neat image to reflect this idea. Instead of talking about the C-Suite, as we used to refer to the team comprised of the CEO, CFO, CCO, etc., we started to talk instead about a Symphonic C-Suite. The 'officers' in an organisation all make a lot of noise. If you listen to their noises individually, that is fine and sometimes even pleasant. But if you listen to them altogether, the result can be a meaningless cacophony. If you want to orchestrate all these different noises into something musical, they need to be better attuned to each other. This requires a different way of working. It may come as a surprise to many of you, but management teams seldom work together, except at moments of crisis. In normal circumstances, they often work against each other, particularly when it comes to securing the budget for their department. But by working together – by aligning the different 'whys' within the organisation – it is possible to turn a cacophony into a symphony. However, the result is not a symphony orchestra, because that would again require a conductor to lead and direct what is being done. A Symphonic C-Suite is more like a jazz band, where every player can do his own solo piece in turn, while the rest of the group backs it up with a solid rhythm. And what if there is a false note? One of the other musicians takes over. This kind of jazz combo stimulates the creativity of all involved, whereas in a symphonic orchestra all the roles are clearly defined within a strict hierarchy. In an ideal world, leadership teams should therefore be much more like the Duke Ellington Band than the London Philharmonic Orchestra!

In other words, it is vitally important to work together during the 'why' phase, in order to determine the right direction of travel. After all, we are flying at 40,000 feet! You at least need to know whether you should fly north or south and which continent you are aiming for. As you approach this continent, you can set your course more specifically. This is the moment when an organisation switches from the 'why' to the 'how' and drops down from 40,000 feet to 20,000 feet. In this phase, the plane will continue to descend further, until it eventually lands. Landing does not mean stopping; it simply means reaching ground level, because in this phase you enter into contact with the organisation. This is when the real change starts. As long as an organisation is still in the 'why' phase, very little happens in concrete terms; it is more about discussion and philosophising, primarily in the heads of the senior management team. This may lead to a change in mindset at the top of the organisation, although to everyone else things seem to carry on as normal. There is nothing wrong with this. In fact, it is wholly logical, since in this phase there is little or no transparency. But that will change in the following phases, when transparency becomes essential.

> **In other words, it is vitally important to work together during the 'why' phase, in order to determine the right direction of travel.**

As the leader, it is important during this phase to take due account of the time axis. In a change trajectory, there are (in my opinion) three axes: who, what and when. Or to express it more fully: is everyone on board, is it a good idea, and is the timing right? During the 'why' phase, ideas need to ripen and this is best done without time pressure, unless external factors demand that change is implemented quickly. For example, it would be pointless to wait another twenty years before launching a self-driving electric car. If it is not possible to align ideas properly within the leadership team, the leader must have the courage to break off the discussions. The timing is not yet ideal. Once again, however, the question is: what kind of leader do you want to be? If you think that you have everyone you need to complete the change trajectory successfully, aligning the leadership team is not absolutely essential. In some cases, it is even feasible to set things in motion with just a single leader on board, but only in organisations where people are accustomed to working as independently as possible from each other. If, however, you need the financial department, the legal team, your customers and other stakeholders to get things done, a decision to push things through without the necessary alignment will only result in chaos.

DUCK FOR LOW-FLYING SLOGANS!

When determining your 'why', you need to make sure that you avoid too much nonchalance. In practice, I often see that many companies devote too little attention to developing a well-constructed 'why' and are inclined to grab at the first catchy slogan that comes into their mind, without giving it too much thought. Imagine that a company wants to cut its costs. There is a good chance that a wider purpose will be attached to this change in a slogan that sounds good but means little, and is intended to blind people to the real motive, which is saving money. For example, you might say that you wish to reduce your vehicle fleet as a contribution to combatting climate change, whereas in reality your main concern is financial rather than ecological. In this (admittedly extreme) case, I would prefer to look at ways of reducing costs in a manner that is credible, while still meeting the company's objectives. If your wider purpose is not authentic, it is better to be honest about things and to say that you need to cut costs because you are lagging behind your benchmark competitors. That is a clear and truthful 'why'. There are then two possibilities to translate this 'why' into the 'how'. You can implement linear cost-cutting measures across the board. Or else you can implement these measures differentially, only saving – but saving more – where there is space to do so. Both options are valid, but the most important thing is to make your story consistent.

Once your direction of travel has been decided, you are ready to close your 'why' chapter and move on. But that is not the end of the matter. During the 'how' phase, organisations need to return regularly to their 'why'. Not to amend it – it is already too late for that – but to check that you are still on course to meet the intention of your 'why'. That is why the first part of the 'how' phase is included in the first circle of our endless figure-of-eight loop. The first task during the transition from the 'why' phase to the 'how' phase is to give shape and form to the change. How can you make it concrete? A first priority is to find a way to measure how your users will be able to cope with the change. Are there existing users? This can either be staff or customers, or both. How do these users use whatever they use? Why should they change? Are they waiting for such change? Will it make their lives easier? Will it also change their status? There are many different reasons for doing something, other than 'because you must'. 'Must' is perhaps the simplest reason for change in a company, but it is seldom the most powerful. Telling someone that he or she 'must' be motivated never works. Compelling someone to be creative might have more success, but not much more. Forcing someone to obey the rules? Yes, that can work. But in each instance this requires the leader impose the change, whereas giving people the necessary space to come to terms with the necessary change is a much more fruitful approach.

" Is it a change that your users have been demanding for the past three years? If so, it will be perceived as a good change and you can push it through quickly. Is it a change that will generate lots of uncertainty, such as fear of job losses? In that case, speed is not advisable.

This is another important aspect on the time axis. Many organisations take plenty of time at board and senior management level to gather information, consult, make compromises, formulate conclusions and take well-considered decisions. Once this process is complete, the direction of travel – the 'why' – has been set. From then on, however, the organisation wants to move forward with the change at lightning speed. Whenever I am confronted with this situation in practice – and it happens quite often – I always say: 'It is wonderful that you, as the senior management team, are convinced that everyone else in the organisation is so much faster and smarter than you are!' If you take a year and a half to allow your ideas to ripen and to formulate an objective, you cannot expect that people who do not have the same insight and perspective as you can complete the change trajectory in six months! That is why it is important to look at your existing users. Is it a change that your users – internal or external, it makes no difference – have been demanding for the past three years? If so, it will be perceived as a good change and you can push it through quickly. Is it a change that will generate lots of uncertainty, such as fear of job losses? In that case, speed is not advisable.

This is the phase in which many organisations fall into the trap of setting up a pilot scheme. On the face of it, a pilot scheme is a fantastic idea: you test out an idea on a small scale and experiment with it before launching it across the entire organisation. But in practice, a pilot scheme is usually incomplete and imperfect. If you then launch it as something fully fledged, its merit as something that has value that can be learnt by all your people is fatally diminished. In that case, your pilot is a charlatan, who offers nothing more than a little occupational therapy for a group of people who evaluate its results (and themselves) on the basis of worthless details. If you want your change trajectory to be authentic, it is better to skip the pilot scheme and start immediately with your main project. Just throw the dice and move around the *Monopoly* board, making your way towards the 'how'.

Sex, money, happiness and death

There are times when you have probably been inspired by a particular form of leadership. That is also the case with the Dutch economist and psychoanalyst Manfred Kets de Vries. In *Sex, money, happiness and death* he not only goes in search of the factors that motivate leaders, but also seeks to identify the lessons in life that they can offer to us. He concludes that for most managers meaningful relationships, making a difference and creating meaning are more important than material matters. Why? Because status is intangible, popularity transient and material wealth insecure.

Manfred Kets de Vries, Palgrave, 2009

2

HOW

WE ARRANGED TO HAVE A GAMES EVENING with a group of friends. Nobody needed much convincing: the competitive ones just love playing games, the non-competitive ones enjoy watching the others battle it out, and the rest just come for the food and drink! That is the 'why' phase. However, anyone who has ever organised such an evening will know that this is where the hard part really starts. In the next phase, you, as the leader of the evening, need to make more concrete the brilliant idea that you had in the 'why' phase. Progress is not guaranteed, nor is ultimate success. It is possible that you might discover that while the 'why' is very clear in your own mind, not everyone shares your opinion about what makes a good games evening, so that it becomes difficult to put your 'why' into practice. The reason for this might be that the 'why' offers too little room to manoeuvre or does not encourage action.

As with the 'why' phase, the 'how' phase can be divided into two different playing fields: the campaign and the personalisation. The questions asked at the beginning of each of the sections below will help you to keep direction. If you can answer these questions easily, you are probably ready to move on to the next stage of your journey around our endless figure-of-eight loop. If, however, you find the questions difficult to answer, perhaps you need to quickly run through the previous stage again, in order to clarify things more fully. The questions that we need to answer in this phase of the loop all begin with 'how'. How will you approach the change that you envisage? During the first part of the 'how' phase, this remains relatively abstract. During the second part, this abstraction will become more concrete. It is important to know that there are number of tools and instruments that you can use to deal with the 'how' phase. These include leadership, HR practices, the setting of priorities, the allocation of resources, organisational structure and supporting technologies, relations, networks and politics, status and symbols, jargon and collaboration. You don't need to use all of them in every change trajectory, but it is nice to know that they are there when you need them.

Let us return briefly to the bank that we discussed in the previous section. We saw that 'making money' is not the most ideal 'why'. 'Making life more pleasant for people' is much better. True, it is not very concrete, but it is at least a 'why' that no one can object to. Your next step is to decide what things might look like once your objective has been achieved. Just as important – if not more important – you need to decide who you are doing it for. For a bank, that might be professional people, organisations or young families. These are three very different groups, each with their own very different wishes and needs. During the 'how' phase, you will need to think how you can best reach and help these target groups and how the personnel in your organisation can help to make this possible. In the business world, making ideas concrete is a major step – and one that often goes badly wrong. It is also the phase in which it is often necessary to protect boards of directors and senior management teams against themselves. These boards and teams are usually filled with people who have little feeling for the daily realities of the organisation, being more used to taking decisions at an abstract level. Which is fair enough, because that is their job. To turn your 'why' into a 'how', you need to involve other groups, from team leaders and their staff to customers and other stakeholders. You need to make the switch from a simple game of *Patience* for one or *Four in a Row* for two to a proper board game like *Wits and Wagers*, where many more players are possible.

CAMPAIGN

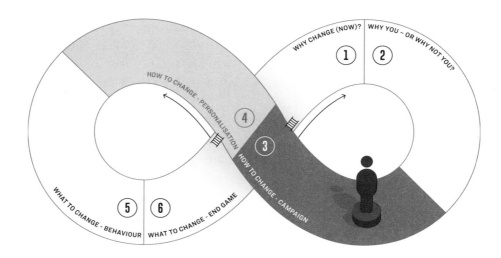

- How will you recognise a 'success'? What will it look like?
- How will you express it in terms of words and results, and to whom?
- How will you justify the resources that are necessary to achieve the objective?
- How do you decide what implicit and explicit resources are necessary in respect of time, budget and scope?

THE DIRECTION OF TRAVEL TOWARDS SUCCESS HAS BEEN SET. We now need to ask ourselves: what that success will look like once we eventually reach our destination? And what do we need to do to make this happen? These are important questions, but it is just as important to know what your own organisation feels about what you are planning. Many change trajectories overlook this, because (rationally enough) they focus primarily on measurable objectives and not on unmeasurable emotions. Unfortunately, measurability is not guaranteed to generate energy. Achieving the financial targets set by your boss is perfectly measurable, but how many members of staff does this make happy, resulting in their better motivation? Not many. If any.

> **" Many change trajectories overlook this, because they focus primarily on measurable objectives and not on unmeasurable emotions. Unfortunately, measurability is not guaranteed to generate energy.**

An important group in this respect are the team leaders, your middle management. This is where bottlenecks frequently occur during change trajectories. Team leaders work at a level that requires them to have partial insight into the abstractions of the organisation's leadership, as well as understanding the daily realities of the organisation as they are experienced by their team members. This means that they are able to recognise if the abstract decisions are likely to work or not, whilst at the same time needing to remain loyal to the senior management. Which also explains why they are the group that is most likely to show resistance to the proposed change. This puts them in a kind of 'no-win' situation, where they can please no one. Those below them in the organisation blame them for pushing the change too hard; those above them in the organisation blame them for not pushing it hard enough. In other words, team leaders are constantly operating in a field of tension, in which emotions play a major role.

Beyond the eight phases of Kotter
—

In the historical overview later in the book, you will be able to read more about the theories of John Kotter and the eight phases through which he argues every change process must pass. For now, suffice it to say that if you want to apply these theories in practice, the moment of transition between the 'why' and the 'how' is the best time to do it. In most cases, the dividing lines between the different phases of the change trajectory are not as clear as Kotter suggests, but his eight phases are certainly useable and, viewed rationally, his 'case for change' is of value. If a leader proposes a change, your first response as an employee is generally a rational one, because the leader represents the employer who pays your wages. In addition, however, you want to know if your emotional 'whys' can also be satisfied. Every employee will be concerned about how the proposed change affects him or her: what will be the impact on his or her status, career, well-being, job satisfaction, learning opportunities, etc. The social context is also relevant. People are attached to their habits and surroundings, even in their professional life. This was clear to see during the corona crisis. What people most missed when they were obliged to work from home was not the endless succession of business meetings, but the possibility of social contact with their colleagues. This social aspect plays a key role in change. The general attitude can often be summarised as follows: 'Do whatever you like, but don't take me out of my social bubble!' People are more inclined to go along with change that they do not like, providing they are left in their familiar environment. If the change removes them from this environment, they are much more likely to resist it, even if they can see that the change is meaningful. If you are used to playing *Cluedo* every Friday evening with the same group of friends, you can probably be more easily persuaded to play a different game with those same friends than to carry on playing *Cluedo* with a bunch of strangers.

In other words, you need to look beyond Kotter and take account of the emotional and social aspects of the situation. In practice, this can be difficult, because many leaders and managers focus exclusively on rational elements, believing that emotional elements are not really their responsibility. Most organisations have a social service that deals with such matters and, if necessary, can even arrange psychological counselling. Managers think that their job is to manage, not to hold people's hands! Is this fair comment? Or not? It depends on the kind of leader you want to be and the kind of leader that your character suits you to be. The extent to which you lean towards the Kotter approach can be a good indicator. The repetitive nature of Kotter means that his system is strongly focused on processes and is therefore more top-down than bottom-up. A good example of this was given to me by my good friend Ivo Pareyns. As the HR director of a large bank, he was given the task of implementing a major restructuring that involved a significant number of job losses. 'The most difficult phase to manage was what I call the kill-your-darlings phase. During this phase, you need to tell people that they can no longer carry on doing what they like doing, the things that they do best and which give them most satisfaction. In the bank, this took up a lot of time and there were many moments when the tears flowed plentifully. But it was time well spent, because it is important to make space for these emotions. The best way to get people on board for far-reaching change is to clearly show them the reality of the situation, to show them an equally clear solution trajectory, and, above all, to repeat consistently your belief that together we can do this. This transparency helps to convince the majority. At the same time, you also need to be equally transparent in your discussions with the minority who cannot or will not follow. Every employee has the right not to accept the proposed change, but those employees have to understand that this means they must go. Even then, you must continue to be helpful and correct, as you guide them towards the exit door. Every change in a company involves a moment of decision. As an employee, you either back the change or you don't. It is one of the tasks of the leader to make clear that this choice – and its consequences – cannot be avoided.'

Intelligent design

—

How are you going to plan all this? Whatever game you are playing (or change you are proposing), you cannot just start without first checking and agreeing on the rules. And what if three players all want to use the same blue counter? You need to have a framework for sorting out whatever problems may arise. During a change trajectory, you need to plan, plan and plan again during this 'how' phase. You are now flying at 20,000 feet, but will soon need to descend another 19,999 feet before you can move into the 'what' phase and make your landing. The best way to descend is in 19,999 equal steps of one foot, but that is seldom possible. This means that process planning will therefore be necessary. This tells you in a formal, business-like manner how to get started and outlines the allocation of resources that will allow you to turn your 'why' from theory into practice.

This planning will be influenced by the extent to which an organisation is capable of change. Imagine that you know an organisation thoroughly and conclude that it is possible for that organisation to move forward by one unit of change each year for the next 50 years. That is the organisation's level of changeability, the amount of change it can absorb. This yardstick is linked to matters such as the number of customers, the level of customer satisfaction, the launch of new products, the speed at which work is carried out, the quality of that work, the room for making mistakes, etc. If, however, the realisation of the 'why' requires the organisation to move forward by ten units each year, the process plan and the willingness of the organisation to change will need to be adjusted according. Another crucial determining factor is the level of change commitment. The higher that level, the faster the change can be implemented successfully. In most companies, the basis for their plan is something like: 'This is the direction we want to travel and we must reach our destination in ten years'. Next, this ten-year period is divided up into a set of annual targets, a straightjacket with which the entire organisation is forced to comply. A pleasanter and often more successful approach is to set the direction of travel and then see how far you get during the first hundred days of the trajectory, taking account of the willingness to change and the level of commitment. Have you already reached the objectives for your first phase? Great! Then you can move on to the next one. Have you achieved more than planned? Even better: you can now increase the pace of change. Have you achieved less? You will need to scale back accordingly. This kind of learning process is essential in a change trajectory. Because every form of change involves learning. You learn something new or you unlearn something old, but at the end of the day it is all about learning in one way or another.

How are you going to design your change? Is it good for society? Is it good for your customers? Is it good for your employees? Is it good for your shareholders? If the answer is 'yes', why have you waited so long to do something about it? If you take the design as your starting point and do it properly, you can be certain that your customers – or some other stakeholder – will be waiting for that change. This means that when you launch it, it must immediately be available for everyone in that target group; otherwise, you will be creating dissatisfaction and a feeling of unfair and unequal treatment. This is a different kind of launch from one where you know that there is going to be opposition

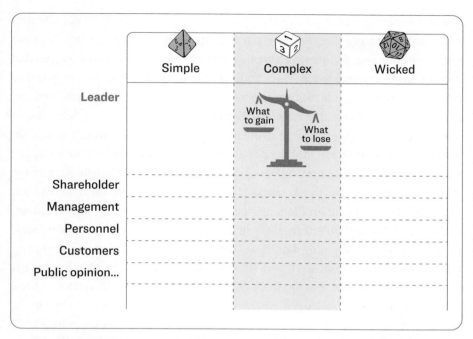

	Simple	Complex	Wicked
Leader		What to gain / What to lose	
Shareholder			
Management			
Personnel			
Customers			
Public opinion...			

For every change it is necessary to assess what will be gained and what will be lost.
After Daniel Kahneman.

and you need to decide how you can break through that wall of resistance. A fascinating book about giving shape and form to change is *Change by Design* by Tim Brown. He explains how you can use design to transform a need for change into a demand for change, within the context of a humane vision that helps organisations to become more creative and innovative. During this design process, you also need to take account of the underlying 'cascade of behavioural choices'. This involves identifying where the choices that need to be made by everyone involved in the change trajectory are positioned. In part, this depends on the nature of the job, but also on the nature of the organisation. Think back to the two receptionists who we met in an earlier section. If a guest asks for something that has not been reserved in advance, the receptionist who works with a predetermined script will need to go to her boss to see if this can be arranged (or not). The receptionist who has more freedom to act independently will be able to deal with the question herself. In this case, two behavioural choices have been made during the interaction; one by the receptionist and one by the guest.

There are many areas and many different ways in which we make behavioural choices. We all have access to modern aids that make our job that much easier, from programmes for sorting through routine e-mails to technologies that help us to get the real work done. You are able to choose how you respond towards each of these aids. Sometimes you use them a little; sometimes you use them a lot. A good example is to be found in the customer services department. Until a few years ago, it was possible as a customer to telephone a company; nowadays, it is a rarity to find the department's number listed on the company website. In fact, it is increasingly hard to get in contact with any human being inside the company. This only works if the company can provide a fast answer to a regularly recurring problem. Otherwise, you risk damaging your customer satisfaction. In our bank example, you could, say, focus on the questions most frequently asked by young families, formulated on the basis of gut feeling, but also by using statistics. How do these families usually react? What are the risks? How, as a bank, can we limit our own risks? You could carry out local tests with products that appeal particularly to young families and then make any adjustments that are necessary before rolling out the trajectory on a wide basis. In this case, a pilot scheme is a creative approach to getting the change ball rolling, because young people in Liverpool or Memphis differ very little from young people in Birmingham or Dallas. In this way, the abstract concept of improving people's quality of life is linked to the financial possibilities of young people in a much more concrete fashion. And by making the change more concrete, you also make people co-owners of the trajectory. It becomes, if you like, their own baby. And no one thinks that their own baby is ugly!

THE LINE OF LEAST RESISTANCE

There is always resistance to every form of change. Except perhaps for longer holidays and more pay. Even then... A good way to reduce resistance is to use a technique that actually comes from Hollywood. The major blockbuster films are first shown to a test public, often in different versions with a different ending. This test public must, of course, be representative of the film's target group. The ending that the test group likes best has the biggest chance of making it into the final version that you will see at your local cinema. There is no reason why organisations should not use this same method during their change transformations, but it seldom happens. The reason for this is the level of involvement it entails. The test public in Hollywood plays an important role in the final decision of the film company. In other sectors, there is a reluctance to concede this much involvement – and the surrender of power it implies – to outsiders, even though it will reduce the level of resistance and increase the likelihood of successful change implementation.

Once again, the crux of the matter is all about the offering of choices. As a board of directors or senior management committee, you need to sketch a framework that provides maximum freedom of choice in the prevailing circumstances. But once you have this framework, it needs to be respected. If the board says we will play marbles, you can shout and scream as much as you like that you want to play bowls, but it will not be possible. If you want to play bowls, you will have to leave and find an organisation where they prefer it to marbles. However, within the framework there will be plenty of space to make a range of choices, such as the colour of the marbles you play with. And the more space you can give, the less resistance there will be. Remember also that the size of space is relative. If you are constantly referring to boundaries, the available space will seem smaller and may even feel claustrophobic after a time. But the more you refer to the space itself and the emptiness it contains, the bigger it will become in people's minds. Because emptiness is something that can be filled. If you focus attention on the limitations of your framework, you will be likely to prompt the unions into a knee-jerk response to push the boundaries further. But if you concentrate on the empty space within those limitations, you encourage energy and creativity. Because being able to give shape and form to your own job, no matter how minimal the choices might seem, gives greater satisfaction.

The certainty of change
—

In recent decades, change trajectories have become an inevitable part of the life of every organisation. In a world that is changing with ever increasing speed, companies have no option but to initiate change after change, if they do not want to be left behind. There is no escape, and so the best thing that you can do is to try and frame the changes positively. How can you do this? By regarding the change as a learning process. Telling an employee that he or she can take part in a change process has a very different effect from telling that same employee that he or she must change. Emphasising that this will involve learning a range of interesting new things has a much better impact than emphasising that nothing will ever be the same again, with all the negativity this implies. As a change manager, you can include these insights in your change design, but you need to do it almost playfully. Learning (as we all remember from school) can be boring. But by turning it into a kind of game, you can make learning fun. Once again, you can use scientific testing to check which approach will bring the best results. Moreover, this also provides the opportunity to further enrich your 'why' phase, but only if you are willing to constantly check that your 'why' is still consistent. This requires a certain flexibility of thought. If, for example, you decide to treat a particular customer segment in a particular way, you must have the courage to analyse whether or not this is compatible with your 'why'. It is important to try and ensure that the 'why' and 'how' phases mutually strengthen each other in this way. Otherwise, there is a possibility that your 'why' will never move beyond the abstract discussion phase.

❞ As a board of directors or senior management committee, you need to sketch a framework that provides maximum freedom of choice in the prevailing circumstances.

The 'how' is the phase in which you move into the world of decisions. In other words, it is a tactical phase in which different pathways are suggested for initiating action and moving forwards. This also means that you must have the guts to say 'stop' if something is not working, so that you can try again with a more effective option. Do you make participation compulsory or optional? Do you encourage people to take part or do you punish them if they don't? That is already four options, and you can combine them to make even more. Unfortunately, most companies have a tendency to think that once a direction has been set, it is necessary to get everyone to follow that direction in the same manner. Wrong! You need to think of it as being a bit like a game of *Ludo*. You can let one of your pieces get half way around the board before you bring your second piece into play and allow it to catch up. And if you throw a six, you check to see which of the pieces would benefit most from a double turn. By trying to make everyone do the same thing, you are actually treating people with a lack of respect for their individuality and dynamism. You often hear it said that it is respectful to treat people the way you would like to be treated yourself, but in my opinion that is false logic. If I know that you would prefer to be treated in a different way than me, why should I try to force you to do things my way? I would then be imposing my view of the world on you – and that is domination.

This is an area where much can be learnt from marketing practice. Marketing works with personas. Everyone has their own personality, which is the ultimate form of segmentation. If you approach everyone as individuals in a manner that matches their personality, this will give you the best chance of getting everyone to jump on board your change train. In practice, this becomes untenable once you start working with larger groups: it is neither feasible nor economical. But if you make use of a generic personality that has sufficient characteristics to be typical and is broad enough to be applied to,

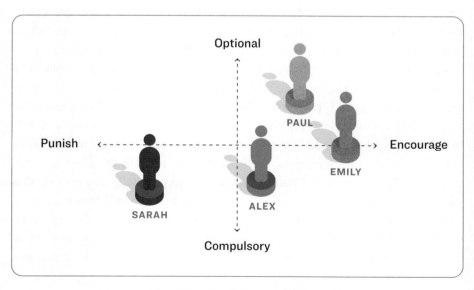

An approach that differentiates change on the basis of personas
significantly increases the chances of success.

say, a thousand people, you have a workable persona. Companies make very little use of such personas, and certainly not when it comes to their internal change processes. They prefer instead to look at departments and functions as the basis for their differentiation: for example, everyone in a logistics function is given the same treatment, everyone in a financial role is given the same treatment, and so on. But all these people have a personality, which is more important as a differentiating factor than their position in the organisation. Some people like change and are keen to test out new ideas immediately, irrespective of role and function. Others prefer a more wait-and-see approach, while yet others are just plain scared. Differentiating the 'how' of your change on the basis of personas will lead to much more satisfactory results than basing it exclusively on roles and functions.

The fact that you cannot treat everyone in the same manner and reach everyone in the same way is evident every time a democratic election is held. This is a subject that has been extensively researched in the United States. What are the main conclusions? People who are uncertain and feel that they have little control over their life are often more easily convinced by making them scared. This is a factor that was played on heavily during the last two American presidential elections. People with strong convictions were appealed to through positive and constructive campaigns. Others were frightened by being told what might happen if 'the other side' won. Applying this theory to change processes, the message would be: 'If you don't play along with change, then…' Whether or not this is a good idea is a different matter. All I am trying to show is that it is not always as simple as saying: 'Everyone has to know X, Y and Z by that date' – which is nevertheless implicit in the generalised simplicity of the ADKAR model. To my mind, change is more about wanting to and not wanting to. That being said, there are still parts of the world were 'wanting to' is a secondary consideration and 'not wanting to' means that you will instantly lose your job. In the West, however, and certainly in Western Europe, those bad old days are now behind us. The important element in the 'how' phase is to ensure that the optional nature of the change gradually disappears. People need to be persuaded to commit. You can do this by specifying objectives and setting agreed deadlines. This creates a 'burning your boats' mindset, an expression derived from the ancient Japanese method of waging war. If you attack another island and burn all your boats as soon as you have landed, you are faced with two stark but simple options: you have to fight and win, or else you lose and die...

AN EMPTY HOLY GRAIL

You can make things too complex, but you can also make them too simple. The popular ADKAR model by Prosci falls into the second category. Many people regard the model as the holy grail of change, but in essence it is nothing more than the principles of marketing applied to the change process. According to Prosci, to allow change to be implemented successfully it is necessary for individuals to pass through the five stages of his model. ADKAR stands for Awareness, Desire, Knowledge, Ability and Reinforcement. These objectives are sequential and cumulative. In other words, you need to follow them in the right order. There is a marketing principle which says that if you are not aware of a particular product or service, you cannot be interested in it. In other words, you first need to stimulate the customer's awareness, before leading him to that product or service. Prosci argues that something similar also applies to change. As the leader, you must first make all your people aware of the possibility of an alternative. Once you have done this, you need to make the change desirable, before using the necessary knowledge and ability to implement that change and make it lasting.

To a large extent, the model is accurate, but by shifting the process of change to the individual level it becomes something that has much in common with the grief curve of Elisabeth Kübler-Ross. There are three problems with this. Firstly, the grieving process does not always run as schematically as Kübler-Ross suggests. Moreover, the grieving process is an individual process, whereas a change process involves an entire organisation or at least an entire department. This means that more mutual influencing can take place. Even more importantly, the depiction of the change process as a grief curve implies that change is a loss or a problem that needs to be solved, whereas current thinking is more inclined to see change as a fundamental part of human existence. In the course of our life we make major choices that bring about great change: going to university, getting married, having children, moving house, and so on. If we would need to go through a grieving process every time we make a choice of this kind, most of us would be likely to limit the number of such choices to a strict minimum. In my opinion, the emphasis – both in the business world and elsewhere – should be placed on the idea that change is about people's own choices. This is what organisational leaders need to make their employees believe: that they have nothing to lose, but something to win. And if you lose nothing, there is no need to grieve.

How to combat suspicion

Early on in the change process, in many companies you can find a dichotomy between the extent to which there is either confidence or fear to share the idea of change with the employees. These two tendencies stand in opposition to each other, like the black and white pieces on a *checkers* board. If there is a bond of trust amongst the employees and between the employees and the hierarchy, there will be a high degree of willingness to take part in the change story. This does not mean that all these people will effectively do what the changes requires, but because their environment feels safe they will at least have positive intentions. If, however, there is an atmosphere of anxiety within the organisation, in the first instance employees will react with suspicion towards any proposed change and they will want to know if it might be used against their best interests. Similar anxiety can also sometimes be felt at the very highest decision-making levels within the organisation, if the proposal for change comes from an external change manager. Trust and anxiety are two important elements that need to be taken into account during the 'why' phase, not only to help determine whether or not the 'why' is justified, but also to decide whether or not this is the right moment for discussing change. An organisation that is dominated by fear and suspicion will not cope well with change, no matter how urgent it might seem.

There are various methods to calm the suspicion and distrust that often attach to change. The two most important are both derived from psychology. For the first, I turn once more to the work of Nobel Prize winner Daniel Kahneman. Kahneman distinguishes between slow thinking and fast thinking in a manner that again forges a link between psychology and work. He argues that our brain and our nervous system react to things in two very different ways. The first reaction is a kind of automatic pilot, as might be the case, for example, when we instantly move out of the way if we see an object hurtling towards us. This system uses very little energy and in the course of millennia of evolution has become an unconscious process. Which is just as well, because if our ancestors had needed to think at length every time they saw a foreign body rushing towards them, the human race would not have survived very long! In contrast, the second system involves conscious reflection about the actions we take, such as learning to drive a motorcar. This system requires the use of much more energy, so it is hardly surprising that nature gave mankind a preference for the first system, since this is the best way to conserve the body's limited energy resources.

" Trust and anxiety are two important elements that need to be taken into account during the 'why' phase.

For the business world, these two different types of reaction offer interesting possibilities: the first system is useful for making patterns and the second system for changing patterns. Applying one or other of these reaction systems can be an important aid for organisations when seeking to implant change in general and behavioural change in particular. If I want you to follow a particular route during a walk, I can achieve this by putting obstacles in your way that unconsciously lead you in the direction I have chosen. If, however, I want you to find the right route by yourself, I need to encourage you to think carefully about which direction you should take at each stage of the walk. If you apply both systems to the storemen we mentioned in an earlier section, whose job is to collect articles sold by a web shop from a warehouse, you will discover that there is a significant difference in efficiency. With the second system, the storeman has to work out for himself the best route to follow, in order to collect all the products he needs as quickly as possible. This requires intensive thinking and takes time. Alternatively, use of the first system could be made by employing another workman in a control room to whisper the shortest routes into an earpiece worn by the storeman, who simply follows the instructions he is given. This requires almost no thinking and takes much less time. The next step would be full automation, with a robot eventually replacing the human storeman. But that, of course, is a different story.

Let's briefly take a closer look at these storemen and the two possible systems for doing their job. At first glance, you would think that most companies would opt to make use of the first system, because it is more efficient and will allow the storeman to collect more parcels per day than his more independently minded colleague. However, there is also a reverse side to this coin. The storeman who only has to carry out instructions is more likely to be affected by burn-out. His job contains no single element that helps to keep his mind alert and provides work satisfaction. The storeman who makes use of the second system might well have shifted fewer packages by the end of his working day, but he will be tired and happy, which will later be reflected in the number of absence days that both storemen take off work. Kahneman suggested that the best solution was to find a healthy balance between both systems. People are not made to engage in conscious thought, all day and every day, but nor are they made to not think at all. The need to find the right balance is therefore something that must be considered in every change process, precisely because there is a general tendency to opt for the system that requires the use of least energy.

" People are not made to engage in conscious thought, all day and every day, but nor are they made to not think at all. The need to find the right balance is therefore something that must be considered in every change process.

The second method that can help to disarm suspicion of change, which again links the domains of psychology and work, is the so-called 'nudge' theory, first elaborated in 2008 by Richard Thaler and Cass Sunstein in their book *Nudge: Improving Decisions About Health, Wealth, and Happiness*. This motivational technique gives people subtle nudges or pushes in a direction that will persuade them to behave in the desired manner. One of the most well-known examples of this is the depiction of a fly on men's urinals, which is designed to encourage its users to aim better and miss less. The same principle is applied to traffic lights in the Netherlands, where a series of smaller 'timer' lights form a circle around the large red, amber and green lights to indicate the moment when the lights will change colour. This simple idea has already significantly reduced the number of traffic accidents, particularly those involving cyclists, who are one of the country's most dominant road-user groups. If we return to our web shop warehouse, it is easy to see a number of potential applications for nudging. I have said it before but it bears repeating: if you include a playful element in your change trajectory, much of the pain that is usually associated with change will disappear, like snow melting in the sun.

Between steering and manipulation
—

Change means that you need to steer people in a particular direction, but the line between steering and manipulation is sometimes a fine one. If you want to play *Monopoly*, you can't really do it on your own. Imagine, however, that you want to play with four people. Your first requirement is to find a second player. That is logical: if you can't find a second, you won't find a third and fourth. In essence, the second player only plays a confirmatory role for the first. You can regard the first player as the leader, the initiator of the game, but only after the second player has made his (or her) appearance. This is an important point: without followers, you cannot be a leader, even if you have that formal title. In other words, if you wish to push through change in an organisation, you must have followers – and that is something that you can stage-manage. It makes no difference who is the first player in your organisation's change game; the second player is much more important. Imagine that you want to carry out a restructuring in a department where twenty people work. It is perfectly possible that your first follower will not be the head of department, but one of the other nineteen. All that counts is that you find the person with the most influence and the most credibility. Is there someone in the department to whom all the others come for inside information. If so, make her your first follower! Is there someone to whom everyone listens when he is telling a story around the coffee machine? Enlist him in your followers' team as well! Once you have got your first two, you can arrange numbers three and four as seems most appropriate, because we know from research that the third and fourth also have considerable influence and impact within the organisation. This is still steering things in the direction you want, rather than outright manipulation, because the trajectory – the story – has been discussed with all four of your followers and they are all 100 percent behind it. This part is actually a relatively simple intellectual process. But it is more difficult to orchestrate what comes next. How are you going to let follower number one start spreading your message and how are you going to get follower number two to take up this message in a manner that strengthens its effect, whilst at the same time linking it with your own credibility? And how are you going to proceed after that? When will be the right moment to introduce followers number three and four into the game? This requires a carefully thought-out tactical scenario, because the timing and the orchestration are crucially important. If you bring number three into action too late, it could ruin your entire change plan.

Another important consideration is to decide whether or not time is a crucial factor in your organisation. You need to assess the importance of time in relation to quality. Can the process be spread over a longer period, because time is not important? How can you influence the available time, so that the change progresses at a certain tempo?

" You cross the boundary between steering and manipulation when you abuse people's credibility.

You cross the boundary between steering and manipulation when you abuse people's credibility. You pick your first four followers based on their ability to have maximum influence within the organisation or the department you wish to change. In other words, they are strategic choices. You may, for example, decide that person X should be one of the four, because he may seem at first to be against you, if he remains silent. This will give his words more impact when he later declares his support for your plan. Once again, however, this is dependent on the organisational culture. In one organisation, remaining silent implies approval of something; in another organisation, it implies disapproval of something. If person X remains silent, this has an important implicit meaning for the rest of the group. It is therefore important for you as the leader of the change trajectory that person X at some point breaks his silence. If the subject of the change perfectly matches person X's own convictions, you are clearly onto a winner: based on his influence within the organisation, you can pick him as one of your first followers with confidence. This still counts as steering the change, without straying across the boundary into manipulation. Imagine, however, that at a later point in the process the nature of the change is extended to include matters that person X is known not to support. If, in these circumstances, you decide to use X as your third or fourth follower, rather than as your second one, this might be considered as a smart strategic move but it does mean that in this instance you will be crossing a boundary that you should not ethically cross. You are now engaging in manipulation, because you are using the credibility of X to push through a change that he does not wholly favour, if at all.

It may well be the case that at first person X does not feel as though he is being manipulated, preferring to rationalise the situation. Moreover, he will gradually take this process of rationalisation further and further, precisely because he knows that he has influence within the organisation and that others will follow his lead, if he recommends something. But in this way, he will gradually use up all his influence credit and his wider credibility will quickly fade away. For me, this is the point at which you have moved from orchestration, which simply makes the music sound better, to manipulation, which uses the music to mask the sound of something more sinister. To make matters worse, you do it deliberately, because you know, as the leader, that people will follow whatever X says. Just as you know that if X continues to support your change agenda, you will eventually undermine his credibility completely. This means taking a step from a healthy dynamic to an unhealthy one. Perhaps your tactics are something like this: 'Maybe X doesn't really believe in the change, but we'll put him up on stage anyway and ask him to do a little dance, so that he at least gives the impression that he is backing us...' This is pure manipulation of the worst kind.

That being said, anyone who thinks that manipulation never happens in change processes is being very naive. On the contrary, it happens all the time; sometimes very obviously, sometimes so that it is hardly noticeable. Again, it all depends on what kind of leader you want to be and within which ethical framework you wish to operate. Even so, it is not always easy to identify the dividing line between orchestration and manipulation, which makes finding the right approach a difficult balancing act for many leaders. Are you familiar with the story of the frog in a pot of water? If you put a frog in a pot of boiling water, it will instantly leap out. But if you put it in a pot filled with pleasantly tepid water and gradually heat it up, the frog will remain in the water until it boils to death. Sometimes leaders face the same dilemma when dealing with their followers. What are we to think of a leader who says to one of his followers: 'You supported the idea during the first meeting, so surely you are going to support it in the second meeting as well? After all, it's your task to get people on board!' If you put your case in this loaded manner, you are clearly manipulating. You could have achieved the same effect with a motivating interview, in which you could use targeted questioning to stimulate your follower's intrinsic motivation.

HOW MANY PARACHUTES?

You could be forgiven for thinking that the number of people involved in a change process systematically increases as the process progresses through its different phases. Let's return to our plane that is descending from 40,000 feet to ground level. In the 'why' phase, you might think that only the pilot and perhaps the co-pilot are involved. During the 'how' phase, the cabin crew join in. During the 'what' phase, the passengers finally get on board. This sounds logical, but that is not always the way it works. The actual level of involvement depends on the leader's ego and leadership style. Leaders with a massive ego believe that they can decided everything alone and will probably attempt to push their decisions through the organisation single-handedly. In other words, they fly the plane solo. If, however, a leader is open to the ideas of others, the plane can already be quite full during the 'why' phase. There will also be more people getting on board during the later phases. Moral? The smaller the ego of the pilot, the more parachutes you will need to have on board!

Saying 'yes' but doing nothing
—

Working your way through a change trajectory is not all that difficult. In fact, it's child's play – as you can see on the cover of this book. As a change manager, I realise that this is not a smart thing for me to say! But there is a snake in the grass that you need to watch out for. And not just any old snake: this one is a real boa constrictor! Organisations, and certainly large organisations, seldom go through just a single change. Usually, there are a number of trajectories, sometimes dozens, running side by side at any one time – a bit like in a game of *Ludo*, where all four counters of the same colour are motoring around the board simultaneously. Therein lies the difficulty and the danger. If you try to pass a large amount of water through a small pipe, at some point the pipe will become blocked. And, for me, change is like that: it is about creating volume. The major pitfall for most changes is that they seldom take account of the wider picture. It often goes something like this: 'This change is for our department, for our team, and it will have little effect on you, but we do still need someone from your team to have a look at few things for us.' Does this sound familiar? For many of you, it probably does. Supposedly, it never involves much work; just 'a few things'. But then other departments start knocking at your door, also with just 'a few things'. Of course, this all adds up, until the workload is so great that your team can no longer do its own work effectively and efficiently. Viewed from the overarching perspective of leadership, the question then becomes whether or not this team should be able to decide for itself which changes it will assist and which ones it will reject. The answer to this question has a major impact on a person's or a team's credibility, because someone who says that he is willing to take part in all changes is not credible. That is just going with whichever way the wind blows.

In practice, this seldom happens. What you get instead is resistance, either passive or active. In some countries the culture encourages people to avoid conflict, even when they are not in favour of something. This results in situations where they search to find the best and least confrontational way to resist. Their solution? Say 'yes', but do nothing. This is not usually intended to be a deliberately undermining strategy, but is based on a genuine concern that there is only so much change that people can take. Unfortunately, it creates a perverse dynamic in which this kind of passive-aggressive resistance can be seriously harmful for the organisation. Consequently, learning to deal with conflict becomes essential. In Dutch organisations for instance, conflict is part of the organisational culture. Discussions around the conference table can be fierce, but around the dinner table they are soon quickly forgotten, with no grudges held.

In all research into top performing teams there is one element that has been shown to be decisive: how do you deal with conflict? With how many of your colleagues can you have serious and even heated discussions about a subject, without it having a negative impact on your relationship? Many people fail to make this latter distinction. If someone puts forward a counter-argument to their proposal, they immediately see this as a threat and assume that the relationship is under attack. This makes further collaboration uncomfortable. If you want to perform at the highest level, making this distinction is therefore crucial. Two colleagues must be able to argue over a subject, be in total disagreement with each other, yet still find common ground to move forward in a particular way that they will both support. This results in an outcome along the lines of: 'We have discussed this, agreed to proceed in a certain manner, and I will follow you accordingly'. And not: 'I am doing what we discussed because I have to, not because I want to, and if I can trip you up somewhere along the way, I will.' For me, accepting the need for conflict and dealing with it effectively is an essential part of any healthy organisational culture. Because if we cannot agree to disagree, we will end up in a debilitating and strength-sapping scenario; a scenario that is a reality in far too many Belgian companies. As a leader, you know the kinds of things that colleague X likes to hear and hates to hear; the things he appreciates and to which he is open; the things that irritate him and set his teeth on edge. As a result, you often end up thinking: 'How can I frame this, so that X will like what he hears?' This is both mentally exhausting and potentially damaging. Because if X is someone who likes to discuss and always thinks he has all the right answers, you still have the problem of finding a way to reach a decision and move forward. You cannot say: 'I am always going to wait until I have convinced X', because it is possible that there are issues on which X can never be convinced. Faced with this situation and the urgent need to make a decision, you must have the courage to challenge X; otherwise, you will end up doing nothing. The question then becomes to what extent this challenge will damage your relationship; your willingness to be open with each other and to collaborate. These might sound like relatively banal problems, but they can seriously poison an organisational culture. That is why an ability to tolerate conflicts is so important. There is an old proverb that says: 'No friction, no shine'. Organisations that allow friction in their culture shine all the brighter.

" **There is an old proverb that says: 'No friction, no shine'. Organisations that allow friction in their culture shine all the brighter.**

Deciding without deciding
—

Earlier in the book, I mentioned the importance of words and the meanings we attach to them. An idea can be non-binding, but it can also be the impulse to launch the right priority at the right moment. These meanings can vary from organisation to organisation, even for a word like 'conflict'. According to the dictionary, it literally means 'a difference of opinion'. But we often invest the word with more serious undertones, above all in a professional context. For this reason, it is important to choose the right word, depending on the context in which you find yourself. For a change trajectory in a Belgian context, it is better to talk about 'a difference of opinion' or 'a different vision', rather than 'a conflict'. Alternatively, you can try to ensure that in your organisational culture the word 'conflict' is not interpreted as harshly as elsewhere. Another word to which it is important – perhaps even more important – to attach the right meaning is 'decision'. In the best case, it means that all discussions have been resolved and there is no going back on what has been agreed. That is how it should always be. Unfortunately, in many companies a decision is a provisional conclusion that will need to be reconsidered in the future, often more than once. Perhaps worst of all is a 'decision' that can be revised after you have started to take action to implement it. Decisions always have consequences and it often happens that people get worried once they recognise what those consequences might be, causing them to reverse the decision in a moment of panic. Decisions of this kind are therefore non-binding, resulting in a change story that is vague and imprecise. Because if a decision is non-binding, it can mean different things. This produces noise – often lots of noise – but very little happens in the way of implementation.

My good friend Anthony Bradshaw is the former CEO of the Allianz Benelux insurance company and now works for the mother company, Allianz SE. When he started his job, he was confronted with the kind of non-binding decision-making mentioned above. 'One of the first things that I changed at Allianz was the habit that every decision, and particularly the decisions of the board of directors, was interpreted as an invitation for discussion. Whereas a decision is, of course, a necessary prerequisite for action. Forbidding all forms of discussion was obviously not the answer, because this has a negative effect on commitment and limits participation. So what did I do? I shifted the position of discussion within the process, so that it now takes place before the decision is taken, rather than afterwards. This means that everyone has to be sufficiently sure of themselves to formulate and express their opinions openly. They are given the opportunity to take part in the discussion, but only at a clearly defined moment. Once the process reaches the decision-making phase and an actual decision is agreed, the discussion stops. Even if you are not happy with the decision.'

The distinction between a decision and a logical conclusion is often misunderstood. Which is a pity, because making this distinction is often crucial. A logical conclusion is often linked to progressively greater insight. With the knowledge and the data currently available, we decide this. But next week (or month or year), when we know more, we may decide something else. Everyone will recognise this form of decision-making as being typical of the corona policies of many governments in recent years. In reality, however, this type of process is not a decision: it is a logical conclusion. Almost everyone else will reach the same conclusion, so that there is no real leadership involved. Leadership is the ability to make use of incomplete information to make assumptions that will allow a course of action to be further pursued. That being said,

CHANGE CAN BE CHILD'S PLAY

leadership can also be a refusal to take an immediate decision, because the available information is insufficient. This is also a legitimate position. But you do not need a leader, if all you are going to do is wait for a logical conclusion to occur. For me, leaders make the difference because they have the courage to take decisions when they do not have all the information they need to feel confident of the outcome. As far as not taking a decision for the time being is concerned, you again need to make a distinction: this time between not being able to and not daring to. Not daring to take a decision as a leader is an admission of weakness. Not taking a decision because you want to gather and evaluate more information is a sign of wisdom and strength. In both cases, the outcome is the same: no action is taken. But in one case this is a conscious choice; in the other case it is based on fear. For this reason, it is important to make your reasons for not taking a decision transparent.

As so often, the kind of leader you want to be also plays a role. If you see the decisions you make as a matter of personal pride, you will not be quickly inclined to reverse them. This means that you will have reached these decisions after careful consideration, with the intention of having them implemented. If this implementation is successful, that will reflect well on you and perhaps also on your pride. A different kind of leader might conclude: 'I am expected to draw a conclusion from the discussions we are currently having and therefore my temporary decision is...' As a leader, the question you need to ask yourself is therefore this: do you want to be someone who takes decisions that people in your organisation do not regard as binding or do you want to be someone who has the courage to take bold decisions, for which you are prepared to take full responsibility?

At the end of this chapter, we have completed the first circle in the double loop of our figure of eight. In an ideal scenario, your change campaign is taking clear shape, so that you can start with its personalisation. If this is not yet the case, you may need to go around this first circle again, because it is possible that your 'why' has not been defined with sufficient clarity.

The art of war

Although it is more than 2,500 years old, *The Art of War*, attributed to the Chinese philosopher Sun Tzu, has lost none of its relevance. It is a guide for leaders and generals who wish to wage war – or run an organisation – intelligently and with success. The book is above all inspirational during the 'how' phase, when you need to devise your strategy for change. In particular, you need to decide whether you will fight in the classical manner, in an alternative manner or in a manner that allows you to win without fighting – something at which modern China excels.

Sun Tzu, Librero, 2010

HISTORICAL OVERVIEW

——

IF, WHEN YOU HEAR THE WORDS *'CHANGE MANAGEMENT'*, they immediately conjure up a picture of men with blow-dried hair, striped blue shirts and a filofax under the arm... you will probably not be far wrong. Much of what we now know as change management and how it is embedded in the business world first developed in the 1980s. That being said, the foundations were laid much earlier. This short historical overview is an attempt – hopefully, a creditable one – to give a chronological survey of the most important doctrines in change management thinking. It does not pretend to be complete: you can find this completeness in other books. Moreover, wrestling your way through this chapter is not necessary to understand the rest of this book. Some of the most famous names in change management history have already been mentioned in earlier chapters. Here, their work and ideas will be placed in a broader historical perspective.

This summary is a useful guide for knowing where change management currently stands, how it got there, and why it has not yet gone far enough. Occasionally, I will refer to other books that offer a wider general survey or provide a more in-depth look at certain phases in the evolution of change management. I will also mention a number of so-called 'standard works', even though I am not always in agreement with everything that they say. So why do it? Because they are widely regarded as expressing 'the truth' and it can never do any harm to have a firm grasp of basic ideas before you progress to more complex theories. Just like a budding artist must first learn how to paint a vase of flowers before he or she can move on to more abstract constructions.

The need to change structures and reflect on the process of how best to do it has been a human activity since ancient times. In the 4th century BC, the Greek philosopher Plato described how an ideal structure (in his opinion) should be constructed – and his ideas are often still invoked today. The same is true of Niccolò Machiavelli, the great political theorist of Renaissance Florence. In his famous book *The Prince*, he explained how a leader can influence and change people. Machiavelli has been dead for over 500 years but his principles are still cited (and often used) by modern-day leaders, not least in the business world, and his philosophy continues to be a standard element in many leadership courses. Many of the philosophers of the Enlightenment also had much to say about change and the nature of progress. So what point am I trying to make? Change management is a very wide-ranging subject, touching on many different disciplines. What it includes all depends on how you look at it.

Programming workers
—

If we are looking for a strict and formal definition of change management, as it applies to the business world, we need to go back to the early years of the 20th century. This is not illogical. The Western world had already passed through two industrial revolutions and stood on the threshold of far-reaching change in many different areas of society. Prosperity was by no means universal, but mass production was starting to become the dominant economic model. This attracted more and more people to the industrial cities, where they lived and worked in the smoke-polluted shadow of the factory chimneys. The working class was born – and, according to the factory owners, it needed to be used effectively. The first theorist to think in a structured manner about the use of labour was probably the American engineer Frederick Taylor (1856–1915), who applied a 'weights and measures' approach to map out its most important fault lines. His rational view of the production process was focused purely on increasing efficiency. His starting point was that workers would always choose the easiest way of doing things and that they therefore needed to be 'programmed' to work more efficiently. According to Taylor, this was possible by observing the actions of each worker individually and then eliminating all forms of wasted time and unnecessary movements. He also made a strict distinction between labour and responsibility. In his view, responsibility was the exclusive preserve of managers; the workers were only required to carry out what they had been instructed to do.

Taylor explained his vision for a scientific approach to the production process in a number of widely read books, of which *The Principles of Scientific Management*, dating from 1911, remained compulsory reading for business leaders for several decades. His ideas had a huge impact on how the emergence of mass production was organised, first in the United States and later all around the world. Taylor was also the inspiration behind Henry Ford's launching in 1913 of the first production line for the manufacture of cars in the Ford factory at Dearborn, in the American state of Michigan. Scientific management became the standard approach for all change processes, adopted not only in production companies, but also by government agencies during the devasting depression years that followed the Wall Street stock market crash in 1929.

" **Taylor's ideas had a huge impact on how the emergence of mass production was organised, first in the United States and later all around the world.**

Thinking about change on a large scale
—

It took until the 1940s before an alternative vision came along to challenge the dominance of Taylorism on the work floor. Its originator was the German-born psychologist Kurt Lewin (1890–1947), who was one of the founders of Gestalt psychology and social psychology. Lewin moved to the United States in the 1930s, where he began to conduct research into group dynamics. He developed what became known as field theory, which argues that people – and therefore also workers – are sensitive to both the inner compulsion of their own wishes and expectations and the external pressure created by the wishes and expectations of others. This idea of 'social pressure' was a new phenomenon in the world of psychology. In addition, his article entitled 'Action research and minority problems' (*Journal of Social Issues*, 1946) laid the foundations for action research. Within this process, the researcher is a social change expert, who no longer just observes, but also intervenes in what is being observed. He guides the desired changes in behaviour and steers people in the direction of democratic values and leadership.

Lewin divided behavioural change into three distinct phases: unfreeze – change – refreeze. This means that people first need to be made aware of their current behaviour and then thawed (or unfrozen) out of their bad habits. Next, they are given the necessary knowledge and skills to make the desired behavioural change their own. Once this behaviour has been successfully learnt, people need to be refrozen, so that the new behaviour becomes an unconscious part of their daily routines. Lewin saw significant benefits in an alliance between the theoretical researcher and the practical expert on the work floor. In his opinion, this was the most important precondition for generating scientific knowledge and advancement. His most important books are *The Field Theory of Learning* (1942) and *Resolving Social Conflicts* (1947). The insights contained in these seminal works made Lewin the first theorist to consider the mechanisms of change on a larger scale. His ground-breaking ideas about organisational development are also still popular in many parts of the business world.

❞ If you want to convince someone to take part in a change process, you need to involve them in it.

The trend for experimentation in the field of social psychology quickly snowballed and in the late 1940s and the 1950s numerous companies took their first steps in this direction. For example, one of the most well-known experiments of this kind was the testing of different strengths of lighting in factory halls, to see what effect this might have on productivity. Following on from this and other similar studies, social psychologists soon reached the conclusion that people are more inclined to display the desired behaviour if they are given the feeling that they have some say in the matter. In other words: if you want to convince someone to take part in a change process, you need to involve them in it. This new wisdom had a major impact on the work floor. The idea of allowing workers a degree of input in some managerial decisions, to create the impression that they had also been partly responsible for those decisions, had previously been unthinkable. For the very first time, participation and involvement became (and have remained) crucial concepts in change management. If your organisation is standing on the threshold of major change, you have two possible options. You can leave it to the management to draw up the main lines of the change process, which are then communicated to the entire workforce. Alternatively, you can harvest ideas for change from every rung of the hierarchical ladder, keeping the best ones and welding them into a change trajectory that will have a broad base of support. Not surprisingly, people will be more inclined to back the second of these methodologies, for which we need to thank the pioneering social psychologists of the 1940s and 1950s.

This was also the period that saw the birth of what is known as organisational development. As previously mentioned, the foundations for this concept were first developed by Lewin (although he never used the term himself). However, it was only after his death that his visionary ideas were followed up on a much broader basis. Tradition has it that the first people to actually coin the phrase 'organisational development' were Douglas McGregor and Richard Beckhard, during the implementation of a management assignment at General Mills in the 1950s. They understood it to mean a change trajectory that is implemented bottom-up throughout the organisation, rather than a trajectory that is forced into one of the traditional pigeon holes that consultants love so much.

Unspoken basic assumptions and their harmful influence
—

A second important pillar on which present-day change management is based was originally developed in post-Second World War London. A group of military veterans – mainly officers – gathered together at the Tavistock Institute of Human Resources, where they were the first to apply the newly emerging principles of the social sciences to business processes, with a particular emphasis on how individuals, teams and groups take decisions. The most important figures in this Tavistock Group were the psychiatrists Wilfred Bion

(1897–1979) and John Bowlby (1907–1990), both of whom had been strongly influenced by the teachings of the Austro-British psychoanalyst Melanie Klein (1882–1960). Bowlby expanded on her ideas, particularly those relating to attachment theory based on the mother-child relationship, while Bion transposed ideas from psychoanalysis into the organisational environment. More specifically, he developed a theory that the behaviour of individuals in a social system is characterised by two different mindsets, which he called the workgroup mentality and the basic assumption mentality. Viewed from the perspective of a workgroup mentality, the task is central, with reality testing and a sophisticated problem-solving methodology providing the answers for anything that is not clear. At the same time, however, the basic assumption mentality pushes individuals towards an almost completely opposite state of mind. These basic assumptions are locked into the head of every individual in every organisation. They are routines, unspoken rules and other matters that seem self-evident. And precisely because these things are not mentioned openly, their influence is unconscious and yet sufficiently powerful to disrupt the desired group dynamics and social systems. According to Bion, it is only possible for outsiders, such as consultants or group therapists, to observe, analyse and interpret this damaging influence. This external help is the only lifebuoy that can save the organisation from drowning.

The humanistic base values of organisational development
—

The concepts of social psychology and the theories of the Tavistock Institute had their greatest impact on business processes during the 1960s. This was when post-war optimism reached its high-water mark, in combination with an increased emphasis on the importance of group thinking. However, this all changed drastically during the 1970s, the decade in which the oil crisis put a serious dent in this worldwide optimism. The business world did not have an immediate answer to this new state of affairs. At the same time, the pace of automation was rapidly accelerating, threatening to change the rules of the business game forever. It was at this moment – in 1972, to be precise – that Newton Margulies and Anthony P. Raia published their book *Organizational development: values, process and technology*, in which they formulated the first humanistic based values for the development of organisations. The six core values are:

1   Give employees the opportunity to function as people and not as elements in a production process.
2   Give every member of the organisation and the organisation itself the opportunity to develop their full potential.
3   Try to increase the effectiveness of the organisation in relation to all of its objectives.
4   Try to create an environment in which it is possible for everyone to find interesting and challenging work.
5   Try to create opportunities for people within the organisation as a way to influence their relationship towards their work, the organisation and the environment.
6   Treat each and every person as an individual human being with complex needs, all of which are important in their work and in their wider life.

As these values show, the world has come a long way since Taylorism.

The emergence of 'change management'
—

It was not until the 1980s and the work of John Kotter that the term 'change management' finally appeared. Kotter argued that it was always necessary to make a case for change. As part of his research, he conducted an experiment at a large international company that made extensive use of protective gloves. He collected together all the gloves purchased by the company's different business locations and displayed them side by side to the senior management. What transpired? There was a massive difference in the prices of the gloves, with some being five times more expensive than others! Kotter wanted not only to show the company that this situation was untenable, but also to create a burning platform for change. His case for change was that it was necessary to review the company's purchasing policy, using a highly process-based approach consisting of eight different steps. Within this process, human beings were regarded as a factor – potentially a risk factor – that needed to be managed. Kotter also introduced a new terminology, much of which is still in use today, such as 'the case for change' and 'the change agent'. Originally, the change agent was a person or leader who had an influence on others, but over the years this definition has become increasingly watered down. Nowadays, a change agent is no longer someone who initiates and implements change, but is more like a canary in a coalmine: someone who picks up and passes on the first rumours and complaints, which signal that problems may lie ahead and will need to be managed.

During the 1990s, Kotter became a kind of oracle in change land. One of his most famous claims was that some 70 percent of change programmes fail to achieve their objectives. Because of his superstar status, this claim was accepted at face value, so that it almost became a kind of self-fulfilling prophecy. Until Paul Gibbons recently decided to take a closer look at the real situation. He first asked an important question: what change are we talking about? Technological change succeeds in between 60 and 70 percent of cases, whereas the figure for cultural change is somewhere between 22 and 25 percent. In other words, it all depends on how you look at it. Kotter chose to look at it in a particularly negative way, which has saddled change management with a harmful reputation and turned it into a cynical – some might even say perverse – industry. Because what can we think of a profession that engages in processes that have serious consequences for many people, but which knows before it even starts that there is a much greater likelihood of failure than success?

Analysing and designing work processes
—

In 1990, Harvard professor Michael Hammer published an article entitled *Re-engineering Work: Don't Automate, Obliterate.* The core of his argument was that all work that does not have an added value for customers should not be speeded up by means of technological improvement, but should simply be eliminated from the process. This strategy of business process re-engineering (or BPR) quickly became very popular as the 1990s progressed. The central element in BPR is the analysis and design of workflow and work processes, with the aim of making them both cheaper and more customer-oriented. As applied to change management, the BPR strategy presupposes that an organisation passes through seven phases before it completes its change trajectory:

- Putting together a change management team.
- Determining a new direction for the organisation.
- Preparing the organisation for the change.
- Creating change teams to implement the change.
- Aligning structures, systems and resources to support the change.
- Identifying and removing obstacles to the change.
- Absorbing the change into the organisational culture.

Hammer believed that his model could be used to push through all change in all circumstances and that no distinction needed to be made between different organisations. In reality, this assumption has long since been undermined, but this has not stopped the model from still being widely used today.

Change management in the 21st century
—

It is only in the last decade or so that behavioural economics has been able to exercise more influence on change management, so that some practitioners now dare to see (and make use of) the link between labour and psychology. One of the leaders in this field is the previously mentioned Paul Gibbons. With his book *The Science of Successful Organisational Change*, he finally brought change management into the 21st century. Based on his many years of practical experience as a change consultant to major organisations, including the British Parliament, he has been able to burst many of the long-standing myths about change management in a manner that allows him to connect human change with organisational change. In this context, for example, he applies the findings of psychological research into behavioural change and cognitive bias to the process of change management.

In the wake of Paul Gibbons, a number of other interesting books on change management and related subjects have been published in recent years. Some have become classics; others are less well-known. It will probably not surprise you to learn that it is primarily works from this second category that inspire me the most. Peter Senge is an authority on learning organisations and I imagine that by now almost everyone has read his remarkable book *The Fifth Discipline*. For that reason I would recommend one of his more recent works: *The Necessary Revolution*, published in 2008. In this book Senge moves beyond systems thinking and looks more closely at moral responsibility and leadership styles. A very different book is *Amoeba Management* by Kazuo Inamori, which offers a fascinating vision on organisational structure that is focused on growth by keeping everything as simple as possible – hence the reference to an amoeba, the simplest living creature known to science. Inamori's vision has been making progress in Asia for the past 20 years and has already resulted in the creation of a series of successful conglomerates, where the culture is diametrically opposed to the need for control that is so common in business circles.

❞ With his book *The Science of Successful Organisational Change*, Paul Gibbons finally brought change management into the 21st century.

The work of the American professor Karl Weick, one of the more esoteric figures in the world of organisational structure, is completely different. It was Weick who first introduced mindfulness into the study of organisations and he also developed the concept of loose coupling, which means that the different components of a system are only loosely connected to each other, so that any change to one component will scarcely have an influence on all the others. His most famous book is *Managing the Unexpected*, published in 2007. For me, a final piece of essential reading for anyone interested in change management is *Breaking the Code of Change* by Michael Beer and Nitin Nohria. At the start of this century, Beer and Nohria brought together academics from many different disciplines to discuss the nuts and bolts of change management. This allowed them to distil a number of innovative new ideas, although (as is so often the case) very few of them were immediately picked up by others in the field. It is only now that their work is gaining the recognition it deserves.

Conclusion? By including an increasing number of concepts and insights from psychology and anthropology into the discipline of change management, we are at last coming to the end of the era of Taylorism. But in spite of this positive evolution, there is still a long way to go: for many, Kotter is still God when it comes to change processes and trajectories.

The Prince

This book by Machiavelli is a true classic, and one that in spite of its age – it was written over 500 years ago – still has relevance not only for the domains of philosophy and politics, but also for the modern business world. Machiavelli illustrates with great frankness the route to power and makes a brutally clear distinction between the rulers and the ruled. That being said, it is often forgotten that in essence Machiavelli was actually a democrat. Although the book has fewer than a hundred pages, for me it continues to be a constant source of inspiration.

Niccolò Machiavelli, Athenaeum, 2019

PERSONALISATION

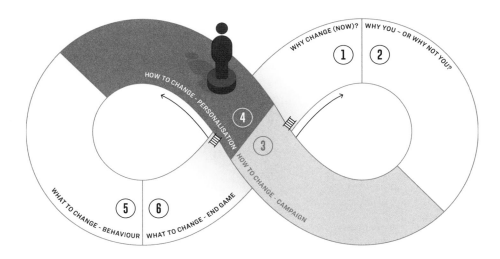

- What is the tipping point and the choice cascade for each target group?
- Are you aware of the (dominant) coalition, the leaders of opinion and the network within your organisation?
- What will you do in the event of resistance?
- Is there room for input flexibility for the team leaders?
- Who has something to win and who has something to lose? And what?

IN THIS SECTION, YOU NEED TO FURTHER PERSONALISE YOUR CAMPAIGN.
Are you familiar with *Codenames*? It is a game in which each team needs to guess words on the basis of (very) short tips and clues. In other words, you need to be able to understand each other with just a single word, which means that choosing the right team members is half the battle when it comes to winning. In this phase of the change trajectory, it is equally crucial to reach the

right people in the right way. During the 'why' phase of our eternal loop, I made comparisons with marketing – and you can do the same with this phase. Setting up a change campaign is not so very different from setting up a marketing campaign. If all the 'whys' in the process are coherent, you are ready for the next step. Should it be necessary, you can go around the 'why' part of our loop a number of times (which is why I have depicted it here again), but at some point you will need to move forwards. If, however, all your 'whys' are not coherent, it will be necessary to weigh up the relevant benefits and drawbacks. In an organisation, you can often find yourself in a position whereby the planned change will not be positive for everyone. Sometimes you will also find that not everyone views the planned change positively, even though it will not necessarily have any negative outcomes for them. These are situations that you need to deal with and you must manage the risks accordingly.

> **Your 'how' at this stage is therefore reduced to this: 'How can I attract the 3 to 3.5 percent of people that I need?' Because that is all we are talking about. Just 3 to 3.5 percent.**

Put simply, you know that what you are planning is not going to be good for everyone, so the task then becomes a question of finding the best possible way to push through your plans with the least possible disruption and damage. How can you achieve this? By setting up what is effectively a kind of marketing campaign to reach and convince the right people within the organisation. Your 'how' at this stage is therefore reduced to this: 'How can I attract the 3 to 3.5 percent of people that I need?' Because that is all we are talking about. Just 3 to 3.5 percent.

Leaders and followers

The classic picture of leaders and followers that has persisted for many years is now starting to become more blurred. We no longer think in terms of a man or woman who sets the direction and leads the way, with a whole group of followers trailing meekly in his or her wake. As long ago as 1988, Robert E. Kelley, a professor at Harvard, developed a model with five different kinds of followership. He pointed out that leadership still continues to be important, but that in the final analysis it is the followers who ensure the organisation's success or failure. The five types that Kelley described are: passive followers, alienated followers, conformist followers, exemplary followers and pragmatic followers. A second usable typology was elaborated more recently by Barbara Kellerman, another Harvard professor. Her model is based on the degree of the follower's engagement and in her book *The End of Leadership*, published in 2012, she argued that the age of the all-powerful leader was over, with this power now passing into the hands of the followers. Like Kelley, she also identified five different types. The isolates have no real attachment to the leader or the organisation. They lose themselves in the crowd and do as little as possible to keep their job. The bystanders carefully monitor the environment, looking to see where improvements are possible, but do nothing to bring these improvements about. The participants make the necessary investment to push through a positive or negative change and are able to strengthen the organisation through their engagement, but they prefer to avoid risks. The activists will actively display like or dislike for whatever is being planned and therefore have a greater share in the organisation than the participants. On the downside, their principled approach can work both ways: they can ensure success but are also capable of dismantling entire systems. The diehards are prepared to make great sacrifices to keep the ideals of the organisation alive and they are extremely loyal to the organisation's leader. Once again, this is a double-edged sword: their motivation can lead to success, but also to the disruption of systems that they regard as being unfair. In this respect, another highly interesting book on the balance in the relationship between leaders and followers is Kellerman's *Followership*, dating from 2008.

As a leader, you need followers, even before you start to initiate change. This means that you first need to identify your possible followers. The good news is that you don't need a lot of them. Research carried out by the American political scientist Erica Chenoweth has shown that just 3.5 percent of the population takes part in protest actions, although this is still enough to topple a regime. Another equally interesting study into behavioural change was conducted in 1965 by the social psychologist Howard Leventhal. He investigated whether or not it was possible to convince a group of Yale students to take a free anti-tetanus injection. He divided the students into two smaller groups, one of which was provided with frightening information about the dangers of tetanus, whereas the other group was given more benign and less graphic information. Logically enough, the first group saw more benefit in taking the injection than the second group. More surprisingly, the number of students who actually took the injection was the same in both groups. More surprisingly still, that number amounted to just a paltry 3 percent. When Malcolm Gladwell repeated Leventhal's experiment some years later, he succeeded in boosting the vaccination level to 28 percent. How? He told the students when and where they could get the injection. Gladwell referred to this simple intervention as the tipping point. Every behavioural change has such a tipping point, a decisive moment when the unexpected becomes the expected and when radical change becomes more than just a possibility and is transformed into a certainty. As a leader, it is your task to find the tipping point in your organisation and its change trajectory.

In other words, you need to convince enough of your people to get on board the change train. The first question that you need to ask is just how wide is your reach as the organisation's leader. In an SME, the leader knows everyone and everyone knows the leader, so that the reach is 100 percent. This is more difficult for someone like Walter Torfs, the leader of the Torfs chain of footwear stores. His company is too large to reach everyone individually at the personal level, so what is the alternative? How can you reach them in a different way? Back in the days of missionary work, the individual missionaries attempted to convert people to their beliefs one by one. This gave them a certain degree of reach, albeit not a massive one. Persuading people to jump onto your change train is much the same as missionary work. It is all about inspiring people to do what you want. You therefore need to know how many people you can reach and how often you can do it. Imagine that you are an assistant in a Torfs shop and you saw Walter Torfs a year ago during one of his store visits. This might have been an impressive and inspirational moment at the time, but does it still inspire you today? Probably not

– or at least much less so. Such moments need to be repeated regularly if they are to maintain their effect. Or else you need to have a really powerful slogan, which can (re-)generate that same effect. Slogans of this kind need to be carefully thought through. It is not enough simply to promise people that everything will be all right. A slogan needs to tell people how you can make a difference on a day-to-day basis. This provides you with an instrument that allows you to connect with them, even if you never meet them personally – which is where the idea of a cult comes into its own. A culture is something that happens to you; a cult is something that you develop over time. Every organisation has an organisational culture, but very few of them consciously cultivate this culture. And it is this conscious cultivation of culture that eventually leads to a cult. For me, this implies both responsibility and a strong action orientation.

As we have already seen, the use of language is extremely important in the business world. What, for example, is 'an idea'? In some organisations, an idea is something that you launch at a meeting but nothing is then done with your idea afterwards. In other organisations, ideas are regularly collected and reviewed. Where questions are raised like: 'Are we now ready to do something with this idea? Is the time now ripe?' The same word – 'idea' – is used in both organisations, but with a totally different approach and meaning in each case. To avoid confusion, make sure that definitions are crystal clear in your organisation.

JOIN THE DANCE

The American thinker and lecturer Derek Sivers once told an interesting story about an amateur film that he had discovered by chance. The film was shot at a music festival and in it you can first see a solitary person dancing alone. His wild, uncoordinated movements have something almost ape-like about them, but this does not prevent a second dancer from soon copying him. The first dancer is now a leader. He welcomes the second dancer and embraces him, sending out a signal that he regards him as an equal. So now there are two leaders. The second dancer calls to his friends and in this way a movement is gradually developed that eventually takes over the entire area in front of the stage. But the most interesting aspect of this film is the behaviour of the first followers. Why? Because they are also leaders. True, they follow the example of the first two dancers, but they do so consciously – and so they lead others to join in as well. In fact, Kellerman's five types of followership can all be applied perfectly to this film. The last dancers are people who follow because it is easy to follow and requires no thought. Just ahead of them are people who follow with a degree of conscious choice but who are still essentially passive, accepting a direction that has been set by others. You can also see that some people are consciously scanning the scene with a critical eye, staying on the fringes of what is happening. In contrast, the active first followers are much more engaged: they are saying: 'I believe in you and the direction you have chosen and I will follow you and your direction as long as that belief remains intact.'

No one can escape the dance

—

Imagine that you want to launch a new brand of crisps. It doesn't matter whether or not your crisps are the best cheese-and-onion, salt-and-vinegar or ready-salted crisps in the world: if you don't get them to the right people, they won't be eaten. Viewed in broad terms, according to the principles of classic marketing, this means that you need to target your crisps at mothers and young people, because they are the largest users and the largest purchase decision-making groups. You can approach this challenge in different ways. If you decide to work through influencers, you first need to know who has the biggest impact on the buyers and eaters of crisps on channels like YouTube and TikTok. Having done that, you next select the best ten of these influencers and sponsor them to recommend your crisps, either directly or indirectly. Another option is to send a free packet of your crisps to millions of mums and youngsters, so that they can taste for themselves just how good they really are. These two options are situated at the opposite extremes of the axis of possibilities, but both take a campaign approach as their starting point, based on the following core question: how experience-based do we want our campaign to be? In this respect, it is important to make the distinction between an abstract phenomenon (a recommendation) and a concrete product (a bag of crisps).

The more concrete the elements in your campaign, the easier it will be to make it more experience-based.

When implementing a change process in an organisation, you can also opt to use this same marketing approach and work through influencers or opinion leaders. In this phase, you will once again need to take into account the possibility of resistance and the need for processes to allow people to come to terms with the change proposals, such as a grieving process. Everything needs to be continually connected to everything else, thereby creating a constant dynamic. In order to identify the opinion leaders within the organisation, you first need to map out the relevant information streams. Who has contact with who and in which direction do those streams flow? Every form of communication is important, both formal and informal, right down to the gossip at the coffee machine. The extent to which you are able to reach this network of the most influential people will determine whether or not you are able to promote your change in this manner. But there are other factors that also need to be considered. Let us return briefly to our crisps example. We had a choice between sending everyone a packet of crisps, to see whether or not our flavours are popular and whether or not they might need adjusting, or, alternatively, sponsoring online celebrities to use their influence to push our crisps in the right places. It is clear that one option will cost more in terms of time, effort and money than the other option, probably to achieve broadly the same result in terms of reach. That being said, the choice you make will also reflect on your image. You therefore need to decide which style you wish to project.

This applies not only to external marketing, but to internal marketing as well. It is like Sivers' story with the dancers. If three of your hundred employees start dancing at the annual work dinner, the dance floor will soon be filled by most of the others. That is why it is so important in every change process to find those three key people who can set the ball rolling. When others see what they are doing, their first reaction will probably not be reluctance. It is more likely that they will feel curious to discover what there is about the process that gives these three trail-blazers such enjoyment and will stimulate their interest to find out what else they can gain from it. Remember, however, that it is not only important that the three demonstrate their satisfaction; they also need to talk about it. In many companies, the latter is more common than the former: there is plenty of talk about change, but little is done to show how things might be done differently to everyone's benefit. This is a pity, because showing that something is fun is much more credible that simply saying that something is fun. So make it concrete. Show how it should be done. Just dance!

Find the influencer
—

More and more companies are using organisational network analysis (ONA) to map out information streams and movements. For example, Microsoft apps like Teams and Outlook are capable of following the connections between different users. This is an extremely useful tool and can help you to track down your influencers in double-quick time. The reverse side of this coin is that a number of the methods for gathering information in this way are contrary to European privacy legislation. One of the things you can do, however, is to circulate an open questionnaire, in which you ask all your people who inspires them most within the organisation. Who gives them energy? Who shares information with them? If everyone in the organisation fills in the questionnaire, or even just a representative sample, there is a good chance that you will be able to identify the people you need to approach. The instruments that you use will depend on the size of your organisation. If you have a club with a hundred members, an extensive network analysis will not be necessary. Any club chairman worth the name will know exactly who is influential with and inspirational for the other club members. And even if you sometimes get it wrong, you can be reasonably confident that whoever you do approach will be willing to join in your story. This is enough to get you started. But sooner or later – and usually sooner – you will probably be confronted by a number of practical difficulties. For example, do your influencers have enough time to do what you want? Because if they are suddenly expected to spend a few hours each day on influencing in addition to their normal work, you will soon find that they are not as enthusiastic as you had hoped! Most of them will end up politely declining any further involvement.

Whatever the size of your organisation and whatever methods you use to find them, the basic rule is to keep your group of influencers as small as realistically possible. There are two reasons for this. First: the larger the group, the more likely you are to intrude on the sensitivities of more and more people within the organisation, so that resistance will increase. Second: within any organisation there are always more people with a follower's mindset than an influencer's mindset. There is nothing wrong with this, and these people are no better or worse than anyone else. The point is that you don't really need to involve them actively in this phase, where their passivity can sometimes do more harm than good. If you have just got out the *Monopoly* board, there is not much value in trying to find fellow players among the people who want to play *Risk*, never mind among people who hate board games altogether! No, as mentioned earlier in the book, you need to identify just three or four key people who can help to get your show on the road. Once you involve them, they will quickly understand what needs to be done and how they can each contribute through their individual roles within the organisation. That is more than enough to get you started.

To find these first followers, conducting a network analysis is often a good idea. Many people think that influencing works in a direct line from the top of an organisation to the bottom: the head of department is the first follower

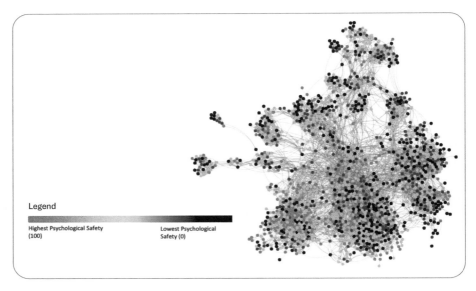

Network analysis provides you with a sociogram of your organisation,
showing not only lines of communication but also the levels of trust between people.

of the CEO, the team leader is the first follower of the head of department, and so on. But things are not quite that simple. In the animal kingdom, it is not always the head of the herd that leads the way to the next feeding ground. In fact, in some species it is the last but one animal that needs to be followed; if the animal at the front strays from the right direction, it is the animal near the back that notices this and carries out the necessary correction. For this reason, herds seldom focus time and energy on the animal at the front, concentrating instead on the animal with the most influence: the one bringing up the rear. A similar dynamic exists within human groups, although the relative hierarchy is frequently less clear. That is why we need to use techniques like network analysis to find out which people have the most influence. In a professional environment, this means asking in the first instance: who do you communicate with? Remember that communication works in two directions. Imagine that everyone in the organisation shares information with me. This means that I am an important communication hub, a clearing house for information within the organisational structure. But that does not necessarily mean that I would be useful as a potential influencer. That is only the case if I, in turn, then share the information I have gathered with others in the organisation who need to know. If everyone shares their information with me but not with anyone else, this probably means that I am the boss. If I fail to pass that information on to others, I am a boss that initiates little or no movement in the information domain.

A second question that needs to be asked in a network analysis is this: who do you follow and who motivates you? Imagine that a large group of colleagues all regard person X as a motivator, even if the change trajectory is a difficult one. In that case, you need not hesitate: enlist him as your influencer. If X says 'Let's go that way' and ten of his colleagues then turn to follow him, it makes sense to invest your time and energy in X – and not in X's boss. Again, it is just the same as with animals: if you can get the first follower to move a little bit to the left or right, a large part of the herd will be able – and willing – to follow more easily. And if we can give person X the feeling that he can also benefit by helping to push our cause, we will be well on our way to generating movement in a large part of our human herd, with the added bonus that they probably won't be thinking too much about where they are going or why.

There is a comparable dynamic in consumer behaviour. If Kim Kardashian starts to use particular products, herds and herds of other people will also start using those products. Not because they necessarily think that they are good products, but simply because they want to associate with Kim Kardashian. Of course, the reverse process is also possible: that people will stay away from the products because they very definitely do not want to be associated with La Kardashian. This is how group dynamics work. It means that if, as the manufacturer, you want everyone to use these products, you will need to employ a number of different techniques. For instance, you must ensure that the people who dislike Kim Kardashian do not get to see the advertising in which she features. Let's take coffee as another example. Imagine that you like to drink coffee, but you do not allow your preferences and your purchasing intentions to be determined by George Clooney, but purely by the taste of what is in your cup. In these circumstances, a coffee seller might be able to reach you by subtly tweaking his blends: a little bit more of this bean, a little bit less of that, until he finds the flavour that is ideal for you. This is now 'your' coffee. And because it is your coffee, it must also be the best coffee! This kind of differential approach is often necessary, particularly when you are working with large target groups. That being said, sometimes you also need to consider just how homogenous you want people's behaviour to be. How much deviation from the norm can you and will you allow?

YOU ARE SAFE WITH US

Research carried out in the 1990s at Cornell University in the United States demonstrated a strong correlation between the possibility of initiating change in an organisation and an atmosphere of psychological safety. This safety is determined by a belief amongst employees that they will not be punished if they express alternative opinions, new ideas or make a mistake. The larger the organisation, the greater the number of levels at which this feeling of safety has an impact. In general, it is fair to say that having access to leadership figures help to strengthen the feeling. The paper for this research was written by Amy C. Edmondson, who went on to further explore this and other related themes in her interesting book *The Fearless Organization*. She takes as her basic idea the proposition that you will get nowhere with your talent in an organisation if the people with the most talent do not have the courage to speak out. Success requires a constant stream of new ideas, but if everyone conforms with 'the way things are' the necessary growth and renewal will prove impossible to achieve. It is the task of leaders to create a space in which everyone can have his or her say, but also where it is acceptable to make mistakes. Again, the same question: what kind of leader do you want to be?

The other rule of three

Most of us will know of the famous 'rule of three' from our maths lessons at school, but in change management there is also another rule of three; or rather, a rule of 3 percent. Some sources say that it is more a rule of 4 percent; other smartasses prefer to stick with 3.5 percent. But the differences are small, so you get the general idea. These percentages refer to the number of people you need to convince in an organisation, in order to get your change process successfully off the ground. Of course, this figure has not been chosen at random, but is based on extensive sociological research, as I have already mentioned in an earlier chapter. Three percent might not sound like a lot, but if you look at social movements in countries where the population runs into tens of millions, you can see that in some circumstances we are talking about quite a crowd! In my opinion, there is a connection here with the tribes in which our primeval ancestors once lived. According to anthropologists, these tribes were never bigger than two hundred people. This meant that the leader of the tribe could have a direct and meaningful influence on his limited number of followers. If the tribes were any larger, the connection with the leader would become less strong, reducing him to a more abstract figure with less authority. If you extrapolate this analogy and apply it to today's organisations, you need to search for the modern-day tribal chiefs that others are willing to follow. These are your 3 percent.

The link between anthropology and the current world of business was explored by the Dutch researchers Danielle Braun and Jitske Kramer in their fascinating book *The Corporate Tribe*. They argue that 21st century organisations are still a form of tribe; that structures are kinship systems; that leaders are chiefs; and that vision texts are totem poles. This led them to put forward a number of surprising insights, some of which are confusing and difficult to accept at first glance, but which, after riper reflection, can nonetheless be used to good advantage in change management. The problem in companies is that authority and influence do not necessarily attach to particular functional titles. Just because you are a director, this does not mean that people will automatically follow you. This is not a problem, as long as you, as leader, are aware of it. It is perfectly possible for everyone to listen politely to the director, but to then look to someone else when they need to decide what and who to follow. In some organisations, this role is played by the unions. If the unions are at odds with the leadership, nothing will get done. The leaders and the unions need to be in agreement before the necessary movement and action are initiated. This can be difficult, but it is also clear. It has something in common with *commedia dell'arte*, the popular form of Italian folk theatre in which every role, from Harlequin to Pulcinella, is fixed. In a similar manner, the unions will use different language when they are talking to the company management than when they are talking to their own militants. But both sides know where the boundaries are and just how far they can go. A union that is always against everything will quickly lose its credibility. So too will a management that constantly depicts everything as being brighter and rosier than it is.

〃 You need to search for the modern-day tribal chiefs that others are willing to follow.

This is a game in which many different emotions act with each other. But these emotions are also linked to status. If, as a union representative, you feel that you are in agreement with the management, but at the same time feel that there is still resistance among your grass roots, you will need to weigh up with which of the two partners you are willing to lose credibility. Will it be the bosses? Or will it be your own grass roots, which has implications for whether or not you will be reappointed the next time elections are held? If you have only recently been elected, you may see things differently than if new elections are due in the next couple of months. This will have an impact both on your status and on your willingness to follow the company line. If you follow, you will drop a rung on the ladder with the grass roots. If you do not follow, you run the risk that the management will think that it is no longer possible to make deals with you. You had an agreement with them, but you did not have your own people under control. For the company, this means that you will fall off the ladder completely! Situations of this kind require a constant juggling act between different elements and emotions, for which the 'whys' in this book can sometimes help to find a solution. What you often see in practice is that emotions triumph over reason. Even if a decision, viewed in rational terms, clearly benefits the grass roots, a potential loss of status many nevertheless push that decision in the opposite direction. An interesting book in this respect is Roger Fisher and Daniel Shapiro's *Beyond Reason*, in which they show how negotiations often transcend the rational level, tipping them over into the domain of the emotions. There is little doubt that they are right on this point – so, as a leader or negotiator, it makes good sense to use your emotions wisely.

THE COMPROMISE: NO ONE GAINS, NO ONE WINS

To avoid a loss of status, we are often willing to make a compromise. In fact, we are often proud of it, because to the outside world it seems as though everyone wins. In reality, compromises often make difficult situations even worse. According to conflict theory, there is indeed such a thing as win-win, but more often than not everyone loses something with a compromise. It is not a disaster, and neither side will bleed to death as a result – but there is no escaping the fact that everyone has lost. If you attempt to find a consensus, you are attempting to reconcile how I can win with how you can also win. This requires more creativity than saying: 'You can either stick to what you want, or we can both do a little water in our wine, in which case we can move further'. This leaves both sides with the feeling that they have somehow lost, while they need to sell to their people the idea that they have actually won something. This kind of compromise is always charged. We have both lost, but there is a good chance that we both think that the other side has lost slightly more. Or the other way around, which means that next time you will be less inclined to make concessions. And the other side thinks the same! As a result, you both end up going around in ever-escalating circles, which threatens to derail the relationship completely.

Emotions on Friday
—

For those who are interested: there are a number of fun techniques that you can use to conduct your network analysis, such as social sensing, which measures emotions, and even text mining. This allows you to assess the nature of your internal communication without actually looking at its content. The tone of our conversations gives a good idea of the emotions we are feeling. Sometimes it is a question of subtle differences, such as a mail that is concluded more abruptly than you might expect or the excessive use of exclamation marks in a text message. Organisations where the use of emoticons is in vogue are ideal for the use of these techniques. Noticing subtle differences in the communication signals that people transmit can be useful in various contexts; for example, when you are playing *poker* – but that is a different story! In a business context, the analysis of emotions can help to determine the speed with which an organisation can push through a change process. If there is currently a positive flow in the company, is that the right time to initiate a change process that you know is going to be disruptive? Do you do it boldly or cautiously? Or not at all? Emotions can help you to decide. Emotional analysis can also help you to make a number of tactical choices, such as when is the right moment to announce bad news. Emotional research suggests that early in the morning is best. Why? Because most people are feeling fairly fresh in the morning, which makes it easier for them to deal with a negative message. But what do most organisations do? They break the bad news on Friday afternoon (usually as late as possible), reasoning that by the time Monday morning arrives most people will have gotten over their initial shock and dismay. Sounds logical? Perhaps – but still wrong. To do this as a leader is highly egotistical. Okay, you have dropped your bombshell, so that you probably feel relieved. But the problem has not gone away: you have simply shifted it onto the shoulders of your people. And they will have to carry it all through the weekend, without any chance to give the news a place or to discuss it with their colleagues. If you do this kind of thing too often, your organisation will soon get a bad reputation – and deservedly so. What many leaders seem to overlook is the fact that they will still need to work further with the same people that they have just treated in this cavalier manner. People whose trust you have just broken. People who have probably been cursing you all weekend. In essence, on Monday morning the leader has to tell them: 'On Friday you heard how things are going to be from now on and even though you may not like it, we are going to need your help to make it possible.' In these circumstances, your employees will probably do no more than the bare minimum that is necessary to keep their jobs. Is that the kind of organisation you want to run? Is that the kind of leader you want to be?

Celebrate your successes
—

The curse of the change manager is that he often joins the game at too late a stage. In many organisations, change management is a label that is added after (or at least half way through) the event, rather like a sticker on a banana. They know what they want to achieve, they have decided what steps are necessary to make it happen and they have made the necessary planning that reflects this. All they now need is to convince their people to play along. This is the moment when they call in someone like yours truly, usually with the message that they have made things easy for me, because all the hard preparatory work has already been done! To which I reply: 'Thanks very much, but you have actually made things much more difficult!' If you have already decided your 'why', 'how' and 'what', all that remains is to sell it to the organisation, but with very little room for manoeuvre for the person doing the selling: namely, me! Working in this way means that it is no longer possible, for example, to develop a participative trajectory, in which people within the organisation can help to design the process. Sometimes things are even worse and the organisation still wants its people to be 'involved', even though everything of significance is already cut and dried. In which case the participative element is purely for show.

What I most frequently come across is a problem with consistency. If everything has already been decided but the idea still needs to be sold to the personnel and stakeholders, the communication is focused on pushing things through, preferably as quickly as possible. The tenor of the message is: 'We have decided everything for you, because we know what is in your best interests'. In other words, a strong top-down approach. That is certainly one way of doing things, but only if it is matched by the content of the process and the kind of leader you are. If you have a superego and are always determined to get things done your way, that is at least consistent. If your 'why' is focused on maximising shareholder return or the survival of the organisation, that too is consistent. But asking in these circumstances how your people can be involved in the process to the greatest possible extent is not consistent. In fact, it is totally out of order. Problems of this kind arise when the leadership of an organisation is not aware that they are in a 'push' story. And if you look at their 'why', you will often see that it is poorly aligned with their 'how'. Another frequent problem is the result of an initial 'why' that is linked to a broadening of involvement. 'We want to start taking greater account of a wider group of people' is a classic that I often hear. On the face of it, there is nothing wrong with that, but if the change is implemented through top-down pushing, the 'why' and the 'how' are totally inconsistent, which means that the entire process is doomed to failure.

> **If involvement is present, the 'what' phase also tends to be very short. Not because something is being pushed through, but because sufficient differentiation has already taken place during the 'how' phase.**

Another important form of consistency relates to the allocation of time. Is the available time correctly divided between the 'why', the 'how' and the 'what'? In most cases, it isn't: there is an imbalance. Some organisations remind me of a group of children who have all afternoon to play, but who spend so much time deciding what to play, why to play it and how to play it, that in the end there is hardly any time left over for actually playing! In a change trajectory, the allocation of time ultimately depends on what you want to achieve. For example, you may have a very good reason for spending a lot of time on your 'why'. Perhaps it is not urgent? Perhaps there are many different opinions that need to be reconciled? But in many more cases there are bad reasons. 'We know that it is going to be difficult and will hit some of our stakeholders hard, so we need to convince ourselves first that we are doing the right thing.' Or: 'We know that this is probably not the right thing to do, but economically we have no choice.' Or 'We'd like to find a way to avoid making this decision, but shareholder pressure is just too great.' In these scenarios, there is usually a sense of being forced to bow to an external factor, which the organisation is powerless to control. It becomes a question of 'must', rather than 'want to'. As a result, the 'why' phase is dragged out for as long as possible. However, this makes no sense. The problem – the need for change – is still there and will not go away. But once the organisation finally reaches this inevitable conclusion, they find that they have a time problem on their hands. Because they have delayed for so long with the 'why', there is no longer enough time to translate this into the 'how' and the 'what'. This creates a kind of funnel effect: the 'why' has taken too long, the 'how' needs to go faster, so that there is not much scope for participation, and the 'what' needs to go fastest of all. This means that what you, as the leader, have been putting off and off and off, now needs to be rammed down people's throats at lightning speed. Once again, is this the kind of leader you want to be? Just as pertinent: do you think that you will get your people to follow you?

The reverse scenario is also possible. In this case, the 'why' is very short, but is repeatedly reviewed during the 'how'. When I see this, I know that a participative process is usually at work. Very occasionally, this might be a sign of uncertainty, which is less good news. But more often than not the basic idea is to create a high level of involvement in the 'how' phase. If this kind of involvement is present, the 'what' phase also tends to be very short. Not because something is being pushed through, but because sufficient differentiation has already taken place during the 'how' phase. The various approaches have been tried, tested and adjusted to reflect the different target groups. As a result, you know exactly which groups you want to reach and can reach, and in which manner. You should never start with people who have a dislike of change. Leave them until later in the process, when you can show that the change is already working. It is even better if you can link this with a successful experience. For example, employee X has already been through the change process and has learnt a new and beneficial way of working. It makes good sense to now put employee Y, who is resistant to change, in the same team as X, so that he/she can also see the benefits of the change. But don't do it too soon: you wouldn't want X to be affected by Y's negativity during the early stage of his/her learning process!

In conclusion: time allocation can be a good indication of the areas to which you want to devote more or less attention. But not necessarily of your reasons for doing so. For example, you might want to keep the 'why' phase short because it is crystal clear that you must do something and do it quickly. But it might also mean that you have a giant ego and you find it necessary to stamp your authority on everything that happens in the organisation. Or perhaps you are just scared of the status quo?

NOT LOSING IS MORE IMPORTANT THAN WINNING

During the 1980s and 1990s, most national football competitions switched from a system of awarding two points for a win to a system that awarded three points instead. The rules were changed because it was felt that the difference between a win (two points) and a draw (one point) was not big enough. Teams found it more important not to lose, rather than trying to win. In other words, they focused on the safer of the two options. The introduction of the three-point system made the riskier option of going for a win more attractive. There is an interesting lesson in this for organisations. If you are initiating a change process, first ask your people what they are likely to lose. Only then should you ask them what they might be able to gain. Why? Because as Daniel Kahneman demonstrated with his prospect theory, people attach more value to loss than to gain. This is also the case in most companies: not losing is more important than winning. This is something that you need to take into account when personalising your change campaign, because every group and every stakeholder has different interests and therefore different things to lose or to win. But when you make this assessment, do not forget that the organisation as a whole is also a stakeholder and that you, as a leader, therefore also have something to lose or to win. This thought is something that you must carry with you throughout the entire process.

Shaping the future together
—

Even the most fervent practitioners of board games sometimes need a break. If, for example, you have been playing *Monopoly* for hours, there comes a point when everyone is happy to slow down the pace of the game or even put the board to one side for a few minutes. But the opposite can also happen. If one of the players takes too long before he throws the dice and makes his move, one of the others might encourage him to speed things up! Likewise, in a change process there is always the possibility to adjust the tempo at which things happen. This can be done at any moment in the process. For example, you might have opted to move the process forward at a constant speed, but unforeseen internal and external factors can always make it necessary for you to put your foot on either the brake or the accelerator. Major events in the outside world often offer opportunities for speeding up your internal operations. The corona crisis was a classic example of this. During this period, countless companies stepped up the pace of their digitalisation and/or the introduction of hybrid working. Why? Often because there was no alternative. Many other organisations took the opportunity to downsize, restructure and review. Not in this case because there was no choice, but because the time and the momentum seemed right. During the Second World War, Winston Churchill once said: 'Never waste a good crisis'. This advice has been taken over and over again during the past three years of COVID. Of course, you don't need to wait for an unexpected crisis to occur. Sometimes you can make use of fixed and predictable events. For example, the presidential elections in the United States are a perfect excuse for speeding up or slowing down (depending on the result). Imagine that you are on the point of launching an American product on the European market and Donald Trump wins the next election. As the company's leader, you may decide that a possible association of your product with the new president is not a good thing. However, breaking off production at this late stage is not an option, so that you need to look at the possibility of slowing things down or repositioning yourself in the market.

Moments of this kind are something you need to consider in advance when developing your strategy for the 'how' phase. What external crises might play a role? What associations might this create? How can you use these associations in your change design? As far as all these matters are concerned, we are living in a fascinating period. It is now clear that corona was a moment to push through changes that would previously have been almost impossible to achieve. Let's look briefly again at the roles of the players in the process during this period. One thing is certain: corona has put the unions under considerably increased pressure. Consider, for example, the increase in working from home. Before corona, the unions were strongly opposed to this development. This may sound paradoxical, but there were a number of reasons for it, some of them good ones. Such as control-related reasons: when you work at home, there is no clocking-in and clocking-off, and no one can see what you are actually doing. How you can monitor and control people is a subject of interest for the unions, but from their perspective this discussion is not an easy one. For example, when people work from home, there is no longer any commuting time. For someone living, say, in outer area of London but working in the city of London, that makes a difference of an hour and a half. In other words, that employee gains 90 minutes a day by working from home. This time has a value, but whose value is it? The employee's? Or the employer's? Most of us would probably say the employee's. However, many organisations reason that this time is something that they have 'given' to their employees, which means that they regard it almost as part of the remuneration package. At the same time, the unions are rightly asking questions about the working conditions in people's homes. In the winter, the heating needs to be turned on for longer, which with current energy prices is no joke. The use of gas, electricity and water all increase. Should staff be compensated for this? Or is the time they gain already compensation? These are fascinating discussions.

It seems unlikely that any organisation had a strategy of waiting for a pandemic before launching home working for their personnel. Companies simply took advantage of the moment: 'This has happened, so how can we use it to make progress on homeworking?' Having taken this basic position, the next step might be: 'It is in our interests that our people work in ergonomically correct conditions, but how can we arrange this?' Fitting a state-of-the-art office into everyone's home is obviously out of the question, so what are the other options? You might, for example, offer people a choice between a company car or a mini-container on the driveway of their house, a kind of fully equipped mobile office. 'But people will need to make a choice', say the company. 'It is either...or, not and...and. We can't afford the extra cost of both. Otherwise, everyone can just come into our office by train. There is still plenty of space and we won't find it easy to sub-let it...' In this way, the focus shifts from staff welfare to cost neutrality. Of course, the unions will remember all the talk about welfare. But they will forget what they have heard about cost neutrality. Before long, you are heading towards a potential stalemate... What is my view on all this? The more you can give shape and form to things together, the more likely you are to be able to reach a win-win situation. In this respect, I differ significantly from the current standard view in the sector. This is probably a result of my youth in Africa, where almost everything seems to be negotiable. Even so, it is an important aspect of any reconciliation or convergence process: what are we going to do together?

If you have completed the two sections on the 'how', you can now move on to the next phase: the 'what'. That being said, it can do no harm to go back and complete the circuit again. But remember what I have already mentioned earlier in the book: continuing to go round in circles from fear or reluctance can only end in tears. At the same time, also remember that your implementation – the 'what' phase – may turn into a disaster if the previous phases have not been sharply enough defined. So don't be afraid to go back to the 'why' and the 'how' – more than once, if need be – to make any adjustments that you feel are necessary. Or to put it in terms of our airplane metaphor: after cruising at 40,000 feet, it is now time to start preparing for your landing. This is the moment to check that you are still following the right course to your destination. During this first part of the landing procedure, your course can still be a general one. But from 20,000 feet to the ground, it needs to be precise. Very precise indeed.

If you take off in Amsterdam and fly to New York, your course will be very clear and exact. But if you encounter wind and turbulence during the flight, you may get blown off that course. Moreover, the wind can come from all sides, so that you need to make constant adjustments. In other words, your course changes during your journey. You are still flying more or less in the direction of New York, but not as precisely as your original flight plan envisaged. Trying to fly directly into a headwind is (tactically speaking) the worst thing you can do. Instead, you need to use the wind by varying your height, speed and direction. You can slip off the direct line to your destination, but never too far. In terms of change, this means that you need to find the right level of consistency to keep you heading towards where you want to go: you don't want to deviate so much that you finally end up in Brazil! True, they do have beautiful beaches, but you can kiss goodbye to that fat contract you were hoping to land in the Big Apple...

The Madness of Crowds
GENDER, RACE AND IDENTITY

This book has nothing to do with change management. In *The Madness of Crowds* Douglas Murray tells the story of the evolution of human behaviour. One of the remarkable things he discusses is the way in which people who have now been living in a democratic system for generations are becoming increasingly intolerant, whereas you would normally expect the opposite. The book is a kind of coda to *The Wisdom of Crowds*, which argued that on average the opinions of a hundred people chosen at random are just as likely to be correct as the opinions of a single expert: a thought that warns us not to overestimate ourselves and our abilities.

Douglas Murray, Bloomsbury Publishing, 2019

3
WHAT

READY FOR AN EVENING OF *RISK*? The board is on the table, the land cards and the armies have been distributed – 'Who wants pink?' – and the players have been given their missions. The experienced gamers will already have a strategy in mind. Perhaps first conquer South America to get more armies, before switching to the main target? But the moment has now arrived for concrete tactics: what are you going to do for your first move? Pass, so that you can position extra armies? Or launch an attack straight away? This phase of the game is the 'what' phase of a change trajectory. We know why we want to change something and we know how we will implement it. Now is the moment to work out exactly what we are going to do. As I see it, there are three important factors that need to be borne in mind.

> **We know why we want to change something and we know how we will implement it. Now is the moment to work out exactly what we are going to do.**

We are probably all familiar with the memory game *I go on holiday and take with me...* You can apply this same methodology during a change process, with the list of things you need gradually getting longer and longer. But in a change trajectory it is just as important to decide what not to take with you. There will always be certain habits and patterns of behaviour that you want to leave behind. This is not always easy. As we have just seen, people find the pain of losing things or leaving them behind is greater than the pleasure of winning things. Viewed from a psychological perspective, it is therefore a good idea to play down what will be lost by the change and emphasise what will be gained. You need to make this dual message as clear as you possibly can, bearing in mind that human beings are intuitive creatures. The American psychologist Jonathan Haidt has illustrated this with a metaphor involving an elephant, a rider and a path. In this metaphor, we are the elephant, which represents human emotions. The rider represents the rational element in life. He thinks that he is in charge, but if it ever comes to a conflict between the two, the elephant will win. The elephant in us follows a path and responds to certain impulses. But at a certain moment a consciousness develops, which says: 'I want to organise my life differently, I want to spend more time on this or that…'. The elephant then follows a different path.

In the context of an organisation, it is usually someone else who gives us a lead and sets our direction of travel. This is formulated as an objective: 'We want to go to…'. Which is, of course, a euphemism for: 'I, as the boss, want to go to…' This direction might be towards an environment where the organisation can be more customer oriented. This, in turn, might mean devoting greater attention to existing customers, but also devoting more time to winning new customers. To achieve this objective, behavioural change will be required. This can also be achieved in different ways. One way is to deal with the change consciously and to keep on dealing with it consciously until your goal is reached. This a bit like trying to stop smoking. Anyone who has ever tried to kick the habit will know that your thoughts are occupied the whole day with 'not smoking'. In an organisational context, this is not sustainable, because sooner or later the elephant is us will come to the surface and we will want to follow our path without having to think too much. This means that we will need to change paths. An elephant is a reasonably intelligent creature, but not overly so. If you lead him along a path that is easy on his feet and does not contain too many obstacles, he will generally follow it without complaint. And it is no different with people in a change trajectory.

I once followed the PronoKal diet. This works in exactly the same way. The various products that you are allowed to eat and drink come with very specific instructions, so that your whole day is mapped out for you. If you follow the instructions and drink your PronoKal mix at three o'clock in the afternoon, your hunger will be stilled and you won't be tempted to reach for the crisps and chocolate bars to see you through the day. The pattern of behaviour that you are expected to follow is detailed with such precision that you no longer need to think for yourself. The only question that needs to be decided is how long will you need to repeat this behaviour until it becomes your new habit.

The 'what' phase also consists of two sections: behaviour and instruments. This last section is also the end game, which allows us to finish our figure-of-eight loop and brings us back to where we first started.

BEHAVIOUR

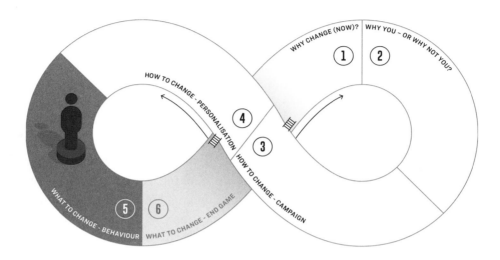

- Do the patterns that you wish to change relate to your identity or your processes?
- Are you fully aware of all your habits and do you know which ones you want to change and which ones you want to keep?
- What instruments do you use to reward or punish?
- Is your journey pleasant?

IN AN ORGANISATION, there are many pleasing and less pleasing instruments that can help you to change patterns of behaviour. For example, the nudges that I referred to earlier in the book allow you to effect change in a relatively playful manner. The key to success is finding the right balance between conscious and unconscious behaviour. People are only consciously occupied with part of their job; there is another part that they deal with unconsciously. This is perfectly normal. We all like the parts of our professional life that do not require us to think too much, because this allows us to keep some time and energy for the other things in life outside of work that we enjoy doing. To make our planned change concrete during the 'what' phase, finding the right balance between the conscious and the unconscious is crucial. The biggest challenge in this respect is to make sure that you do not overdo the rational component, which is what often happens. If you announce that a change is in the interests of the organisation, this is about as convincing as telling smokers that they should stop smoking because it is bad for their health. It just does not work. Patterns of behaviour have little to do with reason and much to do with impulses and emotions. As a result, you do not change patterns of behaviour by appealing to reason, but by making use of reward mechanisms. For many smokers, a cigarette after a meal is about much more than a quick fix of nicotine. It is a moment of pleasure, often shared in informal conversation with other smokers. To break that pattern, you need to find an alternative that is equally satisfying. Otherwise, there is a risk that the reward you are trying to replace will become more and more missed.

A highly interesting book in this respect is *The Power of Habit* by Charles Duhigg. This American journalist investigated why some people can lose weight or stop smoking easily, while others find it so difficult. He also looked at organisations that fail time after time to push through necessary changes, while their rivals do so effortlessly. The key to success – as the title of the book implies – is to be found in understanding the power of habit and how to break those habits by replacing them with other ones.

A second factor that needs to be borne in mind is that in this phase you again need to differentiate. If you take a group of people who want to stop smoking, they will go about it in different ways. A few will be able to stop from one day to the next. They simply decide 'no more ciggies' and are able to implement this decision through sheer will power. A much larger group will need daily encouragement, in the form of reminders about their reasons for stopping, coupled with new rewards that serve as a substitute for their former 'guilty pleasure'. You could, for example, use one of the lists that detail the benefits of not smoking for the human body after number of days, hours, weeks, months and years. As far as rewards are concerned, you could point out the huge cost savings, which could be used instead for, say, a nice holiday.

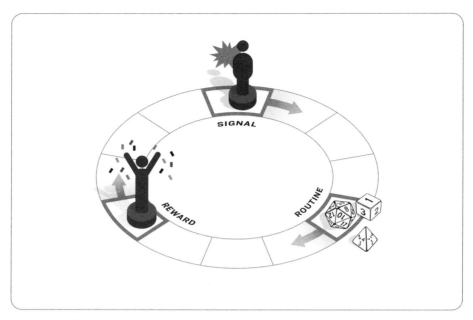

Charles Duhigg's habit loop. Breaking through old habits and replacing them with new ones is the key to successful change.

These methods can also be employed with success during a change trajectory in an organisation. As in the 'how' phase, during this 'what' phase you can also develop 'personalised' programmes for particular personas. This will involve different coaching and guidance measures for people who are more or less well motivated; for people who are more or less attached to status; for people who are more or less influenced by group feeling; and so on. These programmes can even be combined, to take even better account of the personalities of individual employees. The most important thing in all these programmes is that they must give a clear answer to the question: 'Where is my reward?' This is not a rational conversation and certainly not a conversation about what is in the best interests of the company. First and foremost, it is a conversation about feelings and emotions.

It is useful if these coaching and guidance measures take account of the results of recent motivational research. For example, if you give people a certain degree of space to grow and to become better at their work, most people see that 'getting better' as a form of reward. Why? Because it makes their job easier and more pleasant – and let's be honest: few people consciously go in search of ways to make their job harder and more difficult! In addition to providing space, granting autonomy is also a powerful motivator. In each of us, there is a small child waiting to rebel if our boundaries are set so tightly that we feel hemmed in. People who feel that they are not allowed to do anything or contribute anything on their own initiative are difficult to motivate. Once again, however, it is a matter of striking the right balance, because abolishing all boundaries would simply lead to chaos. Think back to the aircrew we discussed in an earlier chapter. Before the flight takes off, this crew needs to explain the necessary safety procedures. Here there is no room for personal initiative: this explanation has to be given in exactly the same way every day. However, there are a number of other tasks that you can give to the crew – putting away luggage, issuing the in-flight magazine, and so on – which give them the feeling that they are not being controlled all the time, but are also able to make a contribution to a positive passenger experience. This latter aspect is crucial. What am I contributing? What difference do I make?

The answer to this question can be a huge motivator, but in many organisations it remains unanswered. This is a pity, because if people feel that they are able to make a difference with a particular task or a particular pattern of behaviour, it becomes much easier to learn and retain that pattern. But as already mentioned: balance is the key. Not setting enough boundaries can be as demotivating as setting too many. If you give people complete autonomy, they may soon feel lost, cut adrift from all help and support. That being said, you can probably take it as a general rule that the more ambitious the 'why' and people's belief in it, the more autonomy you can give. This, however, once again raises the concomitant risk of too much personal input. If every employee is allowed a high degree of personal input and if this input does not match with each other and/or the needs of the organisation, this can lead to confusion and a lack of consistent direction. And because the trajectory becomes increasingly concrete as it progresses through the three phases, this also increases the likelihood that people will find things with which they disagree. Imagine that 'improving people's quality of life' is the 'why' of a company. This is a 'why' with which everyone can agree. But if the company wishes to realise this 'why' through the production and distribution of devices that constantly measure people's heart rate and blood pressure, there is a good chance that they will encounter resistance, because this can be seen as an infringement of personal freedom and privacy. Once again, the solution can perhaps be found in differentiation. If I want control and you want freedom, we cannot both serve the same customers, since that would simply cause confusion. But there is no reason why we cannot divide our customers into segments, so that I deal with the group that is interested in control and you deal with the group that is interested in freedom.

FIX IT WITH CONFLICT

The 'how' and the 'why' in your change trajectory need to be aligned with each other. Let's take a step back to clarify this. The question was: how can we help to increase autonomy? This is a 'how' question, not a 'what' question — which means that when we move on to the 'what', we need to take account of the fact that autonomy is important. This, in turn, means that we will probably need to make use of new technology, but that technology must not be too 'big brother'-like. It must only be able to transmit single signals, based on a number of indicators. This brings us to a very important element in the 'what': conflicts. As I have already mentioned, conflict is negatively charged. However, conflict also means looking at what we can do at the most concrete level, within the limits of our 'why' and 'how', which will allow us to reach our objectives. Conflict brings together your convictions, other people's convictions and your respective levels of autonomy.

At this stage in the process, everything is both tangible and measurable. This is the level at which you do things, but not randomly. It is not a no-obligations testing ground, where you can just try out whatever you want and see how things go. If there is no feedback loop to assess what your actions involve and what consequences they have, you are once again simply indulging your own convictions. What you need is a measuring mechanism that will allow you to analyse and improve. Imagine that you are a specialist in plumbing but want to become an even better plumber. This means that you already have a high degree of autonomy and work relatively independently. That is the nature of your trade. So how can you determine whether or not you are getting better at that trade? Because you are getting more customers? Because you have been able to raise your fees without negative reaction? Because you need to return less and less to the same customers? Because you are familiar with all the latest technical evolutions? This brings us back to the first and most fundamental aspect of the 'what': what do I want to take with me, what do I want to leave behind and what is new? Defining this as concretely and as individually as possible is a huge difficulty for many organisations.

Turbulence on board

In the first part of the 'why' phase, we looked at the two different types of crew members on an aeroplane. We saw that the behaviour of the pilots needs to be as homogenous as possible, with no variation for personal initiative. As we pointed out, we don't want a pilot who wants to show what aerobatics you can do with an Airbus! The norm for pilots is high, but pilots who are capable of doing more than the norm are not interesting for airlines, because they form a risk. Passengers do not expect to arrive at their destination faster than originally planned, never mind that the plane will do several loop the loops along the way! No, the norm is: reliability, consistency and the highest possible level of safety. But it is a different story for the cheaper and less skilled cabin crew. In their case, you do want to stimulate variation, since this is the best way to keep them interested and motivated. This is where airlines try to make a difference, in part because a great deal of what they earn comes from the inflight experience and what they sell on board. This is why their advertising always emphasises the friendliness of their service or the luxury of their planes, and not the dexterity with which the pilot handles the joystick.

Viewed in these terms, it is in the best interests of the airlines that their cabin crew look good and can deal with people comfortably. Why? Because this can have huge impact on customer satisfaction. The behaviour of the cabin crew is therefore more heterogeneous and there is room for variation based on personal initiative, because in this case the consequences of behaviour that deviates from the norm are less dramatic than in the case of the pilots. Imagine that you are an airline and want to improve your customer experience by allowing your people greater autonomy. If you look at your two inflight teams – the pilots and the cabin crew – what do you conclude? With the pilots, there is little room to manoeuvre, because the same safety norms must apply to all of them. You cannot allow a pilot to improvise when it comes to the pre-flight safety checks. Nor will you be able to improve the customer experience via your pilots, because the passengers never see them and only hear them briefly over the tannoy. Even if the pilot does everything 100 percent by the book, the passengers will never notice the difference. Put simply, pilots are not an interesting group for the change process that you wish to implement. So what can you do to improve the customer experience? Sell more things on board? This would certainly be an improvement for the airline, but not necessarily for the passengers. There are very few people who reason: 'During my last flight I bought three bottles of perfume instead of my normal two bottles, so next time I fly it will certainly be with the same company.' No, most people reason: 'During my last flight the cabin crew treated me like a king, so I will definitely fly with the same company again.' This is behaviour that has impact. In other words, the question now becomes: where is there room for autonomy and how do you want to use it? Which behaviour do you really want to see changed?

" The question now becomes: where is there room for autonomy and how do you want to use it? Which behaviour do you really want to see changed?

As in this example, the answer to this question is theoretically easy to define, but it is not always easy to apply in concrete terms. This is one of the major challenges of the 'what' phase, because there is a wide range of other factors that can have an influence, such as the group dynamic. Imagine that you want to change the behaviour of a small segment of your personnel and to do this you plan to make use of the most popular person in the organisation. This seems like a logical choice, but perhaps this popular person is your organisation's equivalent of the Kim Kardashian we mentioned in the consumer example in the previous section. And perhaps that one small section you want to change is the only section in your organisation that does not want to be associated with Mr. or Mrs. Popular. If so, your change process will run into trouble during the 'what' phase. A group dynamic of this kind has inherent influence. I also mentioned earlier how it is sometimes a good idea to get particular people to work together, so that one can learn the desired behaviour from the other. Once again, however, you need to be aware of the dynamic that exists between them. Let's briefly go back on board our aeroplane. One flight attendant is a dream for passengers. Consequently, you want a second flight attendant to learn the same kind of behaviour and so you put them together in the same team. But if both of them have independently-minded characters, so that they both think they know best, they will probably spend the whole flight arguing, so that they don't give the passengers the attention they expect. As a result, you will precipitate the opposite of what you were hoping to achieve. During the 'what' phase, team dynamics are of huge importance, but in practice I often see that this is a matter that many organisations find it easier to ignore.

In change trajectories there is also often a tendency during the 'what' phase to try and implement the change in exactly the same way for everyone. This carries with it the risk that while you might persuade the majority to climb on board your change train, a minority will still remain resolutely standing on the platform. Once again, differentiation is a necessity. This also means that the change must be measurable. Think, for example, of the 'Start to Run' programme, where people's progress is easy to measure and therefore serves as a motivation factor. Because measuring is not only a control mechanism, but also has a motivating effect. Another good example is Weight Watchers. You are engaged in an activity that is not particularly pleasant – watching what you eat – but the use of a points system and constant follow-up transform it from just another dieting system into a stimulus for group change. You submit your points and by the end of the same day you get feedback. These feedback loops are important, because they not only give you insight into your progress but also into your eating habits. As a result, you gradually come to understand that it is your whole attitude towards food that you need to consider. With the

Weight Watchers method, you are allowed in theory to eat anything you want, but you must be aware of the consequences if you do. In other words, their system is less about dieting and more about behavioural change.

In our aeroplane, the job cycle ends after the landing. This is the first moment when feedback is given, usually in the form of a smile and a 'thank you' as the passengers leave the plane. This is therefore also the first more or less measurable moment. If nobody smiles, the flight experience has been extremely poor. If half the people smile, there is still room for improvement. You can create a second feedback moment by asking people to fill in a brief questionnaire. A third form of feedback can be deduced from the growing or shrinking number of passengers that re-book with your airline. If you provide all this feedback to your people, they can do something with it. Which brings us to another fascinating question: 'What are the areas where I can have an impact as a person with my behaviour and the other means at my disposal?' This learning process is inherent in the 'what' phase. Do you remember how in an earlier section we assumed that most people want to perform their work with the least possible difficulty, even in preference to performing their work pleasurably? In short, they want to do their job efficiently and effectively, in a way that will allow them to finish more quickly, but also from which they can learn. In many cases, learning is a motivating factor per se and there are various elements that can be used during the 'what' phase to nourish this learning process, in combination with the networks that you mapped out during the 'how' phase.

Collisions, collisions and more collisions
—

As I mentioned earlier in the section on mapping your networks, the informal communication within an organisation is important. There is, however, a nuance that you need to bear in mind; namely, that in most organisations there is a form of hierarchy. The chance that you will meet the CEO for a quiet chat at the coffee machine is relatively small. CEOs either send someone to get their coffee or have their own machine in their office. Consequently, your communication will tend to be a mix of formal and informal moments. In the past, communication was very much one-way and that one-way was formal and top-down, in keeping with the classic American tradition. As an employee, you were told (not consulted) that your job description and list of tasks was being amended, with criteria that would make a higher variable wage possible, provided those tasks were completed faster. This kind of deal (or rather dictat) was then the norm and in many companies still is. These are highly transactional arrangements, which make clear which job criteria change and which ones remain the same. And if you manage to satisfy one of the variables, you will get paid more. In other words, the reward is money-driven and the whole approach is extremely formal.

In recent years, more and more research has been published which suggests that people are not quite so rational as was once supposed. With formal systems of this kind, negative dynamics soon start to emerge, with some employees regarding it as 'unfair' that other employees earn more for doing the same work. This leads to dissatisfaction and even resistance. If money is the most important motivator in an organisation, you are soon awash in all the emotions with which money is traditionally associated, with greed and envy leading the way. That being said, purely informal systems don't really work, either. It is only the combination of the two – formal and informal – that is effective. Particularly interesting in this respect is the research of Leandro Herrero. Published under the title of *Viral Change*, he examined change phenomena from a bottom-up perspective. Put simply, his theory states that change movements are created at the bottom of organisations, whether they are companies or whole societies. That, he argues, was the rationale behind the Arab Spring in 2010 and 2011: start a movement in which people can find each other, until a moment arrives – like in chemistry – when the boiling point is reached. From that point onwards, the entire chemical reaction is changed.

In the beginning, there will be a number of collisions, but not enough, either in number or speed. It is only when you have enough collisions of a sufficient speed that the system begins to change. This is the point at which the informal side comes into its own. The only reason why so much attention is devoted to the formal side is because it still plays an important role in the allocation of resources. If you want to do things differently within an organisation, but the necessary resources are not made available for the process, you will find yourself with a movement that is ready to act, but will not have the means to become more structural and more systematic.

In our network analysis we mapped out our informal connections. It is in these connections that the change movement often can be hidden. In many of the companies that I visit, it can be painful to lay the map of this informal network over the map of the formal network, because it reveals that the two networks are completely different. In particular, it frequently shows that many of the leading figures who formally have an information-spreading role are not the figures who are regarded with a high degree of credibility in the informal networks. In a formal context, you usually have a boss who announces change from the top. Yet even if the change proposal is fairly concrete, there is a good chance that many of the organisation's personnel will not be convinced. Instead of looking to the boss, they will turn to the people who have authority in the informal network. If they give the impression that they are behind the change and believe in it, the group that first demonstrated resistance will now follow. The motivation behind this change is often gain or self-preservation. Why? Because the reference person in their network is regarded as a reference person precisely because he or she is smarter and more critical than everyone else. The initial doubters therefore know that if he or she says or does something, there is usually a good reason for it – and that it usually results in success. And because everyone wants to be associated with success, it would be stupid not to follow. Because success means more money, more status and more doing fun things. If you are playing *Machiavelli* – a clever card game that requires the use of lots of strategy – for the very first time, your initial reaction will probably be to wait and see what the others do. Later, however, you will start to imitate some of the patterns used by the most successful player, because these patterns seem to be the most credible. But this is not necessarily the player who brought *Machiavelli* to your games evening or even the person who suggested that this is the game you should be playing.

BEWARE OF TOO MUCH ENTHUSIASM!

One of the main problems, certainly as a consultant, is that it is hard to gain insight into these hidden relationships within an organisation. When I ask everyone who has the most influence, this is a very formal approach, which makes it difficult to expose the key informal elements. Few people will be willing to admit that they have no influence – and the higher up the hierarchical ladder they are, the harder that admission becomes. You therefore need to make use of other techniques to approach the problem from a different angle. For instance, you can look at different personality characteristics and attempt to deduce from these who is most likely to have a positive influence over others and who is most likely to be open for trying something new. Some people like to play *Monopoly* every Friday evening, but there are others who are always on the look-out for new board games. They don't yet know the rules, but are still keen to try them out, because that is their nature. People of this kind do not grow on trees, but they exist in every organisation. The secret of success is to find them. In contrast, many more people think that 'new' means something painful, which will lead both to greater confusion and to more work. Their first question is always what this 'new' can do for them. These are the two extreme positions on change willingness, and there is a whole range of gradations in between.

Who, as a change manager, should you be looking for? Is it the person who thinks that everything new is fantastic? Possibly not, because what if this enthusiasm later wanes, so that he or she never finishes what they have started? Colleagues who want to do their jobs better, make their work easier and gain more satisfaction from it know better than to follow such 'experimental' trail-blazers. Why? Because they are not certain that these enthusiasts will stay the distance. And if it transpires after three months that the new idea will not work because its first advocates are no longer interested, the sceptics will be able to claim that they were proven right and were wise not to step on board the change train. As a result of which, resistance to the next 'something new' will be all the greater. No, the person who you do need is the person who is known to favour innovation, but also has a reputation for seeing things through.

'They' are big and 'I' am small
—

When it comes to change trajectories, is there a difference between big organisations and small ones? Size certainly plays a role in terms of the personal or impersonal nature of the process. In large organisations, it inevitably makes more sense to use certain aids and techniques for change, because the leadership is not acquainted with everyone in person and even the employees do not all know each other. In very large organisations, people in one department have often never met people in some of the other departments, never mind know what they do all day. In these organisations, the use of instruments like network analysis is therefore justified. In this respect, it needs to be remembered that the size of an organisation can change over time; for example, as a result of rapid growth or mergers. Equally, the perception of size can also change. Alix Rombouts, the ex-colleague I mentioned earlier, did this consciously at one of her previous employers. 'Our company has employees who started off in an SME that grew and grew until it became a large multinational concern. But they never truly appreciated just how big the organisation had become, because the departments were strictly separated. We opened up their eyes to this new world by having staff from Belgium follow training courses with staff from Slovenia, Russia and South Africa. This made it possible to accelerate a number of necessary changes, because suddenly the idea that "I work for a small company and don't need to be interested in these things" was replaced by a more international perspective. To underline this perspective, we decided to make English our standard language for the company's communication.'

In smaller organisations with, say, a hundred or so personnel, you have the impression that everyone does know everyone else. For this reason, people will be less open to the use of techniques such as network analysis. Whenever I suggest this, I frequently hear in response that it is not necessary and that the organisation itself will tell me who has influence and who does not. Sometimes they are right, at least in part, but more often than not they are wrong. Over the years, it has struck me that this illusion of knowing everyone and every dynamic in the organisation often goes together with very forthright views on leadership. If I ask them how they want to change, the answer is: 'I am the boss, so things are going to change because I say so, and if people don't like it, they can go and work somewhere else!' A healthy 'what' is usually based on the idea that, as a leader, you want to see your people and your teams grow. But this confronts you with the paradox of that 'go and work somewhere else'. The better an employee is able to perform his or her job, the greater the risk that he or she will leave your organisation for pastures new. An employee who does not get better in his or her job and only carries out what he or she is specifically told to do by the boss will find it more difficult to fit in to other organisations. But is this what you really want? I once heard a joke in which a financial director asked a CEO why he continued to invest in the development of his employees, if this increased the risk that they would leave. To which the CEO replied: 'What if we don't invest in our employees and they decide to stay!' There is more than a grain of truth in this.

This touches on something essential. What is the perspective for working together to create something new, to the benefit of all concerned? Every collaboration has an intention and a temporal aspect, spread over a broad spectrum. The intention is not always contained in the paper contract that every employee receives, but more often than not is rooted in a psychological contract. In addition to the legal agreements that the employer and the employee make with each other, there are also other expectations attached to the collaboration. For example, employees expect to be treated fairly and with transparency, while employers expect the employees to be available for work at the agreed hours and when needed. In short, there will always be a mix of unwritten expectations on both sides, which is different in every organisation. Starting a change trajectory impinges on this psychological contract. The employee might have reasonably expected that working for you would be pressure-free, with plenty of room for autonomy. You now tell him or her that things are going to be different from now on. If the employee cannot place this change within the framework of the psychological contract, the change will be resisted. If, however, the psychological contract implies that the employee will be able to learn a great deal from you and your environment, but that in return he or she will adopt a flexible approach to his or her employability, this immediately gives you more room for future manoeuvre. Alternatively, a psychological contract might be based on an understanding that the employee will be trusted to do the job without undue hindrance from the employer, providing the employee does not make an unacceptable number of mistakes. In this case, asking the employee to do something new increases the likelihood that such mistakes will occur, which is not compatible with the psychological contract.

A psychological contract is not necessarily a personal agreement. The larger the organisation, the more impersonal the contract will become. In a government department with thousands of civil servants, each and every employee will have a psychological contract, but this contract will not have been made with the head of that department, who they almost never see. Instead, large organisations of this kind try to set these contracts at the level of the team. At the team level everything is more personal. Team members are the people who you chat with at the coffee machine, discussing the latest football results or how the kids kept you awake again all last night. This emotional connection creates a climate in which there is a greater chance of implementing change. It is a cliché in the business world that if a team gets behind something, this also increases the level of individual commitment. And like most clichés, it is largely true.

What can you do to create more space for co-creation? Because the more you can give people a feeling of co-ownership for elements of their work, the more those elements will truly belong to them. One of the interesting aspects of the 'what' phase is the different types of ownership that exist, since these differences will help you to determine which tactical approach you need to adopt for which people. If, as an employee, you feel that something – say, a task – is yours because you are obliged to do it, but without knowing why, you are probably not the kind of person who is keen to seek ways of improving yourself and your performance. In fact, there is a good chance that you are someone who is simply carrying out a fixed procedure. Some other employees are what is known as outliers. These are people who have a natural reluctance to follow fixed work procedures, but prefer to 'do their own thing', which can be motivated either positively or negatively. The negative outliers fail to follow the procedure because they like cutting corners, or because they are lazy, or because they just can't be bothered to do things properly. The positive outliers are curious to analyse the process and its objectives, and are not afraid to deviate from the procedure if they can find ways to improve its efficiency.

It is interesting to look at these two extremes a little more closely, because in most organisations the majority of methods and procedures are indeed fixed. If your organisation has too many negative outliers, you need to use

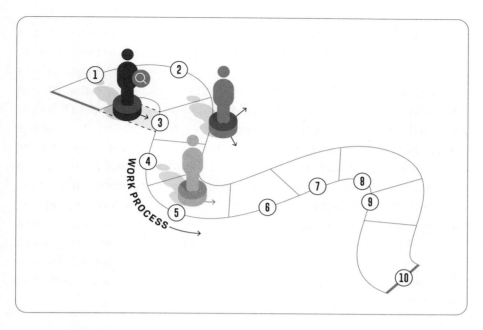

In every organisation there are people who follow the process, people who cut corners and people who improve the process by creating shortcuts.

your authority to keep them in line, using punishments and/or rewards to persuade them to follow the norm and to do things the right way. Positive outliers also fail to follow the norm, but at the same time they also display a high degree of learning potential. Imagine that a process consists of ten steps and you, as an employee, can see that the overall completion time would be faster if you start preparing step three while step one is still active. Consequently, you decide to make the necessary change. Like your negative colleagues, this also means not following the agreed procedure, but it results in a more efficient and an easier way of working. So how, as a leader, do you then respond? If you have any sense, you will discuss the change with the employee and turn it into a learning process that can be shared with others. It is the same when you are playing *Monopoly*. There are some rules that everyone follows – for example, no one will start travelling around the board the wrong way – and some rules that many players ignore, such as the auction rules and the rule that forbids a player landing on the 'free parking' square from picking up the 'pot' accumulated from fines and other penalties. It irritates me that this possibility is explicitly excluded in the rules of the game. In my opinion, it would be better (and more fun) to give the players the autonomy to decide for themselves. This applies equally in organisations. Imagine that a company wants to cut its costs. As the leader, there are two ways that you can do this. You either can introduce strict rules that set a tight maximum budget for each department, supervised by two senior officials who need to monitor and approve every item of expenditure. Or else you can ask everyone to be more economical in their use of resources, offering rewards for those who save the most. The first option attempts to force people to comply. The second option gives people a degree of autonomy that encourages them to comply in their own manner. At the end of the day, both options may result in the same amount of savings, but with the second option you will create a happier and more co-operative workforce. Once again, this a matter of leadership style. What kind of leader do you want to be? With which style do you feel most comfortable?

A change can also be static: 'This is what we have to do and we have to do it now. Please confirm when you have followed all the necessary steps.' There are very few people who gain satisfaction from following an instruction book. Moreover, it offers no scope for learning. This is only feasible where there is room for autonomy and a degree of personal input. It is the extent to which people can invest something of themselves in a fixed procedure that determines the extent to which a learning process is possible. When this happens, change is not static, but is the start of a new learning process. In such cases, change works as a motivator.

It is the extent to which people can invest something of themselves in a fixed procedure that determines the extent to which a learning process is possible. When this happens, change is not static, but is the start of a new learning process. In such cases, change works as a motivator.

This is the point in the trajectory at which you have to decide where to place the focus of your learning process. Is it on curiosity and discovery? Or is it on efficiency and ease of performance? This is a complex matter, because ideally you also want to take account of all the different personalities and personas. However, you will soon realise that this is not possible: there is no single solution that will be good for everyone. Consequently, you need to make choices. How you will develop this or that change process in concrete terms? What will you take with you on your change journey? Some processes will be prescriptive and regulatory. If there are certain legal provisions that have to be respected when concluding a contract with a customer, you cannot say that it is acceptable to temporarily push the law to one side. There is no scope for showing personal initiative when dealing with the law, so that those involved are like rats in a labyrinth. This results in almost Skinner-like situations, with punishment for those who deviate from the right path as a method for conditioning the right behaviour. It is difficult to think in terms of rewards, because there is nothing in the process that can be altered or improved. If, however, we are talking about customer satisfaction or innovation, then there is more room for putting something of yourself into the process. In instances of this kind, it is important not to think too much in terms of definitions and scenarios, because this might limit the autonomy that you wish to promote. In this model, there is room for rewards and it is possible to develop a number of motivating reward mechanisms. This is another area where I increasingly see a shift from the individual to the team level. As a team, we are faster and more efficient, complete tasks more quickly, derive more pleasure from those tasks, and have more time to have fun.

BE THE CHANGE YOU WANT TO SEE

One of the recurring themes throughout this book, and perhaps the most important one, is that leaders must never stand alongside or above change. You must be involved in it and respect its logic. Can you really expect that all your people will carry out everything in accordance with fixed procedures if they can see that you are doing the opposite? This would create discongruity within the organisation. Change management also has to be a change process for you as a leader. It will not work if an organisation wants to cut costs, but the CEO sets no limit on his own expense account. It will not work if a company wants to switch to a greener vehicle fleet for its staff, but the managing director continues to drive around in his diesel-powered convertible. No, there are better ways to do things. At the brewing giant AB InBev, the CEO once said that he wanted every employee to behave like he or she was the owner of the company. To underline his point, he said: 'If I had to pay the fare myself, I would no longer fly first class or business class'. And so he didn't. From then on, he flew economy class instead. If the big boss can give a signal of this kind, it shows that the desire to achieve a goal – whether it is cost cutting or improving the environment – is more than just talk. It also implies action at all levels. This makes the change more credible and is an immediate and massive step in the direction of success.

Where I most frequently encounter obstacles is in organisations that are trapped inside mechanistic systems. A mechanistic system means that everything is locked into fixed structures, because – like Kotter – it regards people as risks that need to be managed and controlled. You can achieve a much better balance by allowing human impulses into those structures, so that being distracted or making mistakes becomes possible, but so does being more creative. Nowadays, there is a growing tendency to speak in terms of living systems. A bee is a fragile creature, but if you unite lots of these fragile creatures in a swarm, you create a potent force. But how can you then direct the speed and power of this kind of more organic system? It is here that the leader, as so often, needs to play the crucial role. The extent to which you are able to improve yourself and your ability to lead changes will also enhance your organisation's ability to change. After a time, this will mean that when you conduct new network analyses, the network of influence will increasingly come to reflect the hierarchical network.

Singapore Food

I love cooking and eating, and because my work requires me to travel all around the world I have had the opportunity to try many difference cuisines. This book by Wendy Hutton not only inspires me in the kitchen, but also when I am dealing with change management. *Singapore Food* was the first book that fully mapped out the rich complexity of that island's cooking. Like many Asian countries, Singapore has a strong tradition of street food, but what makes the Singapore variant so unique is its mix of diverse influences, resulting in fusion avant la lettre and an unlimited willingness to experiment. This has an inspirational effect – at least, it does on me. You can experiment endlessly with herbs, spices and ingredients – and you can do exactly the same in your organisation, seeking to find the right blend of processes, procedures and structures. Dare to move away from the well-trodden path. Who knows? Perhaps you will end up in a more wonderful place than you ever imagined.

Wendy Hutton, Times, 1979

THE END GAME

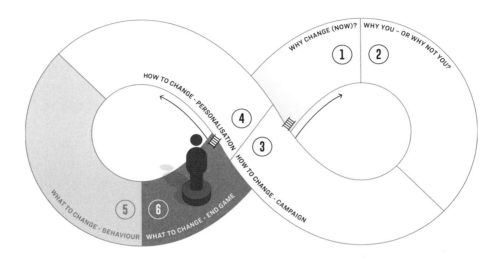

- ■ Are we there yet?
- ■ Are we making progress and how can we know?
- ■ Are we sticking to the plan?

WE ARE ENTERING THE LAST BEND IN OUR LOOP. The finishing line is in sight, but that is when things can start to get difficult. It is just like in a game of *Snakes and Ladders*. You are in the lead and it looks like you are about to win. Your counter has avoided the last snake and you only have three squares to go, but this means that you need to throw a three with the dice. In other words, one chance in six. If you throw less than a three, this gets you nowhere; it simply means that you need to throw a one or a two next time. Again, one chance in six. If you throw more than a three, you might find yourself back on the snake... When organisations reach this second part of the 'what' phase, there is often a feeling of: 'We're there! We've made it!' In reality, of course, there are still lots of things that can go wrong. This is also the moment when motivation can start to flag, because even though the end is in sight, somehow it never seems to get any closer. As the leader or the change manager, you suddenly find yourself in the role of Papa Smurf. People are constantly asking you: 'Are we there yet? Is there still a long way to go?' The first time you answer: 'Not far'. The second and third time, too. But by the fourth time, you are starting to get irritated and snap back: 'Yes, a bloody long way!' This is understandable: the journey has been long and the leader is tired, because in spite of all his best efforts there are still people who have not boarded his change train. What's more, he is starting to run out of ideas about how he can convince them. This reaction is perfectly normal, but what counts now is how the leader deals with it. Are you the type of leader who is transparent about your own emotions? Or are you an iceman, who never lets his feelings show? Or perhaps you are someone who, in spite of your tiredness, continues to press forward and to motivate. In this final phase, it is important to remain alert and to check for a final time that your 'why', 'how' and 'what' are still properly aligned. Because even though you have already invested a lot of time and energy in your change process, there is still time to stop or change your plan, if you deem it necessary.

Puzzling with satisfaction
—

For me, there are two extremes in change. There is change based on binding rules and regulations, which make it unavoidable that you have to work in a particular way. Think back to the example I mentioned earlier about hygiene in the food industry. If you want to sell your hamburgers and have people eat them, you must respect the hygiene legislation. If you fail to (or are unwilling to) follow the relevant regulations, you will have to stop trading. It doesn't matter whether you like it or not. And in this case, it is not an option to try and find a creative alternative solution. No, the rules are the rules and they have to be followed. It is as simple as that. What you can do, however, is to try and add a playful element to your procedures that can keep your personnel motivated. People like games and playing, so that the addition of a lighter element will probably give them a boost. Okay, this might be little more than a diversionary tactic, but it is based on a principle that was known even in Roman times. Give the people what they want: bread and circuses. If you can do this, there is a good chance that you will keep them happy.

At the opposite end of the change spectrum stands the customer, who is constantly searching for a little something extra. We have become an experience society. Whether they pay for it or not, people today want an experience. Everywhere and at all times. Organisations can use their creativity to make these experiences personal and deeply human. Technology tends to standardise experience, while I (or you), as an individual, can personalise it. Depending on what you want to achieve with your change, this offers a huge opportunity. An opportunity that almost becomes a form of change in itself.

> ## " Children who are conditioned to search for solutions derive satisfaction from that search, irrespective of the result. That is the difference between a growth mindset and a fixed mindset.

Once again: you can try out this 'something extra' in a safe manner as part of a learning process, so that you can test the merits of the change, exactly like in an experiment. Let's return to our aeroplane. The basic idea is that when passengers board the plane, everyone gets a free biscuit. Great, you get 'something extra' before you have even taken your seat! Perhaps you'd like a cup of coffee to go with it? In other words, the airline's chances of selling coffee immediately increase. You could test this out initially with just a single cabin crew team. Does it work or not? Does the idea need to be adjusted? This is concrete and measurable. If you see that the system works, you can extend the experiment to a number of teams. This is how a learning process works. Or, alternatively, as the CEO of the airline you could reason: 'We are smart people, so we are going to decide here and now to give free biscuits to everyone on all our flights. And we will tell our cabin crew that by a certain date they have to sell a certain number of additional coffees.' These are two completely different approaches to achieve the same objective, but one is based on compliance behaviour, while the other is a learning process that can be continually adjusted.

Another factor that needs to be borne in mind is that the working day is not only defined in terms of time, but also in terms of satisfaction. Everyone wants to go home after a full day's work, but everyone also wants to go home with a feeling of satisfaction for what they have done during that day. This satisfaction is highly personal. So how can an organisation stimulate this satisfaction process, consciously or not? This brings us to the difference between a growth mindset and a fixed mindset. Growth mindset was a term first used by Carol Dweck, an American researcher who has worked primarily with children. In one of her experiments, she divided a number of children into two groups and allowed them to solve puzzles with different degrees of difficulty. Both groups were given the same puzzle and a certain amount of time to complete it. Once the time had expired, they were asked whether they wanted the next puzzle to be more difficult, as difficult or less difficult. One group of children were given feedback about whether or not they had solved the puzzle and were congratulated for their smartness when they did. The other group was given no feedback about the result, but were encouraged for their effort and the way they had tried to solve the puzzle. In other words, the feedback for this group was more clearly focused on the learning process. How did the experiment conclude? There comes a point when every child is no longer able to solve the puzzle it is given. How do they then respond the next time they are asked whether they want a more difficult or an easier puzzle? The children who were given feedback about their ability to find the result tended to ask for an easier puzzle. Why? Because the reward element in the feedback is focused on successful completion, and there is more chance of solving an easier puzzle next time around. In contrast, the children in the other group tended to ask for a puzzle that was as difficult or even more difficult. Why? Because the reward element in the feedback is focused on the act of searching, rather than on successful completion. In other words, these children have been conditioned to search, rather than to find, and it is from this process of searching for solutions that they derive satisfaction. That is the difference between a growth mindset and a fixed mindset. And it is something that you can teach adults, as well as children. So try out different things in the context of a learning process, to see if you can achieve this same effect in your organisation.

Jumping higher than you can

—

At the individual level, you are in a continuous flow; you have a certain capacity for everything that you do. You can do all these things with various degrees of competence, ranging from not at all to complete mastery, almost like in the old guild system. Imagine that you can skate, but not brilliantly. If you want to improve, you need to match your current capacity level against an appropriate challenge level. Finding the right combination of these levels is the key to success, also in change management. If you practice, you will become a better skater, so that you can make the next challenge even harder. In this way, you make progress and move forward. The important thing is to maintain an optimal combination of your capacity and challenge levels. When you can do this, your experience of time becomes different. You are now 'in the zone', a term that is also often applied to top sportsmen and women. The optimal motivation zone is at the point where the challenge is just a little bit higher than your ability. If the challenge is not great enough, you soon become bored and there is a good chance that your motivation will fall away. And even though you are more than capable of completing the task in hand, you will possibly start making more mistakes than you should.

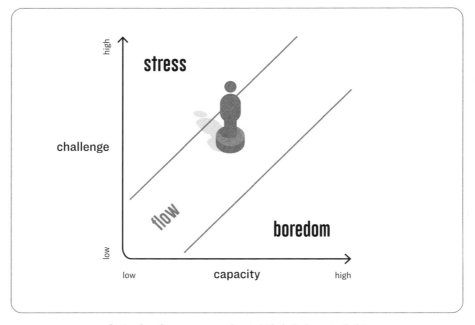

Optimal performance according to Mihaly Csikszentmihalyi

However, this process also works in the opposite direction. Imagine that you can skate just enough to avoid falling over all the time. If I then register you to take part in a skating competition, I would be challenging you at a level that is far beyond your capacity. You would probably find this frustrating and your motivation would be damaged. You need to keep the balance between the two zones at the right level. You can do this by improving your capacities, because this will allow you to take on harder challenges. But you can also do it by adjusting the nature of your challenges, providing you don't take things too far. This interaction is used in organisations as a method for helping people to reach their optimal level of performance, which has the additional benefit of helping them to lose (in part, at least) their awareness of time. You all know the feeling: you start doing something and after what seems like an hour you look at the clock, only to discover that three hours have gone by. When this happens, you are in the zone of optimal motivation capacity. Conversely, if you start something that you don't want to do or is too difficult for you, the minutes seem to crawl by like hours! This mechanism is a fascinating one, because you can use it for the conscious development, maintenance and stimulation of all your capacities.

Unfortunately, this ideal zone can sometimes suffer from interference. We all have things that irritate us and interfere with our day-to-day working, but these things often remain unspoken. If you can identify and remove the routines and rituals in your work environment that do not make a positive contribution, you will soon increase your level of job satisfaction. But this is not always easy. Many organisations, even large ones, often have much in common with the old wife's tale which says that you should always cut off both ends of a sausage before frying it in the pan: nobody knows why it should be done; it's just the way it has always been done. Perhaps this gives a sense of comfort and recognition, but it can also be an interference. If you then want to initiate a change, you find yourself trapped in a field of tension between the comfort that you are now disrupting and your desire to save time and increase efficiency. If you can use this knowledge to positively change these balances, you can give people both more time and more space. Technology, such as the Waze GPS-app, can help you in this. Imagine, for example, that you track someone with a GPS throughout their working day and that you also link this to a stress meter and a heart rate monitor. By the end of a week, you will know whether that person feels better in the morning or the afternoon. You will also know for which tasks their heart rate is low and their level of concentration optimal, and vice versa. With this kind of data, you can plan your employees' work programmes in the most efficient manner. If someone clearly feels better in the morning, set him or her the most challenging tasks before lunch! You can even play with biorhythms in much the same way, which is possible in many jobs where there is a degree of flexibility involved. The aim in both cases is to make the best possible use of the available time, but also – and even more importantly – to increase job satisfaction.

One of the mistakes that occurs in most change programmes is that they do not go any further than the immediately possible. The desired behaviour is known throughout the organisation, everyone has shown that they are able to deal with it – and that is where it stops. But that is not the end, because the new behaviour has not yet become a habit. A habit is only a habit when you start to do it unconsciously. A change trajectory, certainly if you are working with adults, seldom goes beyond showing something and explaining it. Imagine that an organisation has been analogue for quite a long time, but during the home working of the corona period underwent rapid digitalisation by introducing its people to the use of Microsoft Teams. Suddenly, telephoning, sharing files and holding meetings were all carried out by this single app. What most organisations then do is to ask someone (either internal or external) to demonstrate the app and show how it works. 'Everyone understands? Great! Let's get on with it!' This is fine for the people for whom this approach offers the right combination of challenge and capacity. But if your ambition is for something more, there is a need for guidance and instruction that can improve this capacity level. If this does not happen, the new behaviour will not become a new habit. On the contrary, most employees will quickly fall back into their old ways.

A large part of the 'what' is concerned with behavioural change and the follow through. The follow through is how you allow a learned movement to become a spontaneous movement. The timing is very important in this 'what' phase. You are engaged in a purely tactical operation, focused on concrete implementation. Picking the right moment for maximum effect is your main objective.

This moment will be included in your advance planning, but you need to be flexible on this point, if the momentum of the situation requires you to adapt. A momentum can be either positive or negative. A customer who is extremely satisfied and who voluntarily makes publicity for something that you want to do creates a momentum that you can use. 'Look how satisfied that customer is with us!' you tell people. 'Wouldn't you be just as satisfied if you give us a try?!' This is a momentum on which you can build, a momentum that allows you to do something you have been thinking about for the past year but only planned to implement at a later date. Using momentum in this way is a tactical choice that needs to be weighed against the tight planning contained in your strategy. Imagine that an organisation has planned a particular change for March. Why then? Because in January everyone is busy with 'New Year' activities and in February something else first needs to be completed. March is therefore the right time. However, this is a strategic choice that takes no account of the psychology of the moment and the context. If, for whatever reason, a positive momentum is generated in February, like the praise of the satisfied customer just mentioned, it would be foolish to stick too rigidly to your strategic planning. Instead, it makes much more sense to use that momentum to speed up your implementation.

On the other side of the coin, a negative momentum may mean that you need to slow things down. There is no point initiating behavioural change on the office floor if half of your personnel are unexpectedly off sick as a result of a new wave of COVID infections, no matter what it says in your work planning. In other words, it is a trade-off between artificially fixing the timing for something over a period of, say, two or three months and accelerating or decelerating the timing in the face of good news or bad news, and using that news to change the dynamics of the situation. To express it in cynical terms: if one of your best friends dies from cancer caused through smoking and I try to convince you to stop smoking by emphasising the dangers it involves, I am not appealing to your reason. I am simply making use of what has happened. You can attach all kinds of motives to events in this way, but if it is your intention to encourage change in a particular kind of behaviour, this tactic creates a momentum for that change. Whether this specific example is ethical or not is another matter!

Leave the biscuits alone!

In every work rhythm there are moments that are more important and less important. If you wish to push through change in an organisation, you need to take account of this. One of the first lessons you are given by experienced change managers is that you can change everything – everything, that is, apart from the biscuits put on the table during meetings! These must be left alone, at all costs! Sounds crazy? Perhaps – but it is also true, and it demonstrates an important aspect of business life: the important moments in an organisation are often to be found at a ritual or emotional level. One of my clients once made an analysis which showed that his company spent 120,000 euros each year on free coffee. That is a lot of money. The rational solution would have been to ask each member of staff to pay 10 cents for every cup of coffee they drank. In that way, my client reasoned, coffee would be cost-neutral for the company and still cheap for the employees. Perfectly possible, of course, but before you do it you need to know whether coffee moments are important within the organisation. In organisations where drinking coffee tends to be an individual activity, those moments are less important than in organisations where teams hold a collective 20-minute coffee break. In this second instance, the coffee moment is a ritual that strengthens the bonds between team members. In other words, it is a moment in the working day that people value. If you attach a negative connotation to that moment by asking for money for the coffee, you will create resistance – and lots of it. In the company where I used to work, there were six different kinds of free soft drink in the drinks machine. One day, the number was cut from six to two. For me, this was a disaster! Okay, rationally I knew that I had been spoiled for choice in the past and that having two kinds of free drinks at my disposal was still a luxury. Even so, I was furious. This shows that taking things away from people, no matter how seemingly inconsequential, is always a sensitive issue. So, as a leader, make sure that you always know the value of what you are taking away. How important are these things and moments? And can you replace them by something else?

Consider, for example, office printers. If everyone in an organisation has a printer on his or her own desk, this encourages a waste of paper. As a result, many organisations now have just one central printer on each floor of the building. This has a number of advantages. People think twice before they print something off, because they first need to walk to the printer. At the same time, you also encourage them to walk more, which is healthy. A central printer is also a social place, where people can meet. These moments might mean that your use of paper per printer falls less than you had hoped, but you can make this good by adding an ecological motive to the equation: 'Let's all try to use less paper, because half the things that are printed off are never used!' In this way, you create a collective ambition. To support this ambition, you can position your remaining printers at points that cannot be seen by everyone during their work and also introduce a badge system. Someone who still prints a lot will perhaps need a gentle reminder that the aim is to reduce paper use, but in this way you involve him or her in the effort to achieve something together. Sometimes, you can even add a play element into the change – 'Who has the lowest print score this week?' – which provides a second form of motivation.

By taking account of the different ways that people are motivated and combining them, you can create a broad stimulus for your change plan and ensure that people encourage each other to realise it. The problem in many cases is that organisations fail to give the necessary attention to this in advance. It is crucial to know your important moments. You can also create new important moments to give an added boost to your change trajectory. The working week, certainly for an ordinary employee, is made up of a fixed number of hours when you are assumed to be working. Some of these hours give you no feeling of emotion; you have simply done your job. Other hours are perhaps spent in meetings where hardly anything of value is said and you get the feeling that your time (and everyone else's) could have been better used. But then there are a few moments each day that really give you energy. The coffee break can be one of those moments.

It is even possible for you, as the leader, to make these moments yourself; moments that help to move your organisation forwards, while also improving the job satisfaction of your employees at the same time. For example, you can organise a weekly team moment, during which you share the highlights of the last seven days. Or a weekly moment when you discuss the best and worst experience with a customer. Or a moment when you talk through the biggest blunder of the week. Sharing blunders in this way can create a truly powerful moment. Most organisations find it hard to admit their blunders, preferring to sweep them under the carpet and pretend they never happened. This is a mistake. Sharing a blunder can be a valuable learning moment that also helps to boost confidence and trust within the organisation. It sends out a strong signal: 'Blunders happen and we learn together how to avoid them.'

" Change must be a part of people's life and work. If you can make this possible, you create the dynamic that is necessary for successful change.

Once you have discovered these moments and given them more attention, you can gradually use them to soften and explain the negatively charged elements of your change trajectory. For example, you might be able to link the 'blunder of the week' moment to an external 'why' like legislation. Applying legislation, especially new legislation, is always an inconvenient and tedious change for an organisation, but if you can infiltrate it into an important moment, perhaps you can take off its hard edge and make it almost seem like fun. 'Where have we applied this legislation least well this week?' You can discuss this in the group, with no blame and no punishment. This allows you to create a valuable team and learning moment that can be used as a lever for the necessary change. As a result, you make the change easier. Change is often seen as being difficult because it is something artificial. It gives people the feeling that not only are they living their life and doing their job, but now also have to deal with change on top of everything else! No, this is not how it should be. Change must be a part of their life and work. If you can make this possible, you create the dynamic that is necessary for successful change.

HAPPY WITH AN APP

We are all dependent on apps. Lots of people love them. So why shouldn't we use apps to help push through a change trajectory? For example, there are various apps that warn travellers against the dangers of dehydration. If you fail to drink enough, you get a warning bleep from the app, telling you to hydrate. You need to enter various parameters into the app, so that you are consciously active with matters like your energy level, food, drink, and so on. The result is better overall health. A similar app could also help you in a work context. If your general health is in order, the good moments at work become even better and the bad moments perhaps less bad. Okay, you are spending time on a number of techniques that have nothing to do with your work directly, but they do have an impact on the wider work environment and your experience of how you deal with it. With this in mind, the apps will give you tips about the best way to keep your energy level and your emotional level under control. As a result, changes will seem less burdensome.

Comfortably rusting
—

A misconception I regularly hear is that new employees are more inclined to go along with change and learning processes than their more long-serving colleagues, who have become part of the organisation's 'furniture'. This is not necessarily the case. It is true that new employees need to undergo a fairly steep learning curve, but this is inevitable, simply because they are new to the job. But this does not mean that their motivation level is any higher. On the contrary, research has shown that people's motivation levels are not at their best during the first year of new employment. This is because you are learning to adapt to new techniques and a new organisational culture, which is not always straightforward and can sometimes lead to frustration. And frustration has a negative impact on motivation. Even so, the motivation in this first year still remain fairly high, and thereafter it rises still further. In fact, dependent on your personality, it continues to rise on average during the first three years and only then starts to decline, although this can also vary from person to person. This is the moment when the challenge level becomes more important, because this is a difficult time in anyone's career. You now know everything that you need to know to do your job. You also know the organisation and have made its culture your own. As a result, you start to feel bored. Perhaps this feels comfortable for a while, but if you learn nothing new, you will gradually rust into complacency and eventually start to make mistakes.

Do you remember how earlier in the book we discussed the time I played *Magic: The Gathering*? Lots of players (including me) developed a strategy, refined over several months, to secure the right cards that could win them the game. Once this strategy had been finalised, they stuck to it time after time. Initially, they were sometimes successful, until other players came along with newer and better strategies. The early winners were no longer able to adjust and gradually faded into the background. To avoid such moments, organisations often employ a system of job rotation. Having finally reached your peak of performance after three years, you are probably not looking to switch to a new job immediately. But if you don't do something new between the end of the third and the sixth year that stimulates you to learn again, there is a risk that your performance will decline. This 'something new' does not have to be a completely new job. It is possible, for example, to retain 90 percent of your current job, combined with 10 percent of other duties that are a match for your challenge and motivation levels. This creates a kind of mini-curve, where your performance first drops a little and then rises back again. If you can repeat this kind of arrangement regularly, you will never rust into decay. But you need to be very aware of just how much you like doing what you are doing. Unfortunately, most people fail to do this and fall instead into a pattern of familiar behaviour. Why? Because it feels so comfortable. Few people have the courage to step voluntarily out of their comfort zone. The vast majority need to be prodded out of it with the right stimulus. And when personal change is involved, there is an added complication. You might think that you have left your comfort zone because you are trying something new, but if nobody notices the difference you are still actually in your comfort zone. So what have you achieved?

The creation of an optimal field of tension between capacity and motivation should be normal practice for each employee in every organisation. But it isn't. In fact, it hardly ever happens. What do you generally see? People start sliding down the motivation curve but the management fails to intervene, because at this stage the necessary work is still being done to an acceptable standard. As a result, the number of mistakes start to pile up and the employee's level of job satisfaction hits the floor. When this point is reached, the typical response is to look at the cost of the employee in relation to the contribution he makes. Yet still no action is taken, because dismissing people is also an expensive business. Switching the employee to a different job is also not considered, because he has shown during the past five years that he is no longer capable of learning. This is an unhealthy situation for all concerned, both the employee and the organisation. In the end, but much too late, it is finally realised that dismissal is the only option, unless long-term sickness intervenes first, and the responsibility for this sad state of affairs is laid exclusively at the door of the employee.

In most cases, you can avoid this doom scenario if the employee can be pushed further up the motivation curve. But who needs to initiate the necessary action to make this possible? As an organisation, do you create enough learning opportunities and room to manoeuvre for your people? Do you leave the initiative for doing something new to the employees in question or do you, as the management, ask them to do something? This is not all as straightforward as it sounds, because at the moment when action is necessary you are dealing with an employee who is at the top of the motivation curve, is working well, hardly making any mistakes, and demanding very little attention. Even so, this is still the right moment to ask what the next step for this employee should be, even though he will probably want to carry on doing what he is currently doing for as long as possible. In this situation, it is the leader who holds the key; a leader who can sense dynamics, recognises individual needs, and has a positive impact on how the employee experiences his job. You can compare it with a teacher who is able to make a subject more interesting or less interesting for the pupil; the basic subject matter – or the job – remains the same; it is the human dynamic that makes the difference.

One of the most interesting of these dynamics is how it is possible to continue learning at a suitably adjusted tempo. We know that the motivation curve starts to turn downwards after an average of three years. However, this varies from person to person and perhaps also from job to job. Imagine that you are an accountant and that you like being an accountant. What's more, you are a stickler for correctness and every figure has to be accurate, right down to the last decimal point. In your case, it is possible that you will not need a new challenge after four years, but only after ten or fifteen years. Of course, during that period you will still need to stay up to date with new legislation and new bookkeeping systems, which will push up your motivation curve slightly. In other words, finding the right balance is an exercise that each individual needs to make for him or herself. Be aware, however, that this potentially creates a problem at team level, because if every team member is doing something new, the leader will quickly lose control of the situation.

PUSHING THE BOUNDARIES WITH A HACKATHON

An interesting technique to use during the 'what' phase is a hackathon. This is an event during which teams deal non-stop with concrete cases, in an effort to find workable solutions. One of the most well-known hackathons in recent years was held by the energy sector, and petroleum companies also launched an innovative contest to collect new ideas to make the earth a more 'energy-healthy' place. It was ironic, perhaps that petrol companies should come up with this approach, but it was a clever move and one that strengthened and improved their image. The huge advantage of a hackathon is that it allows you to gather lots of ideas in a quick and direct manner, and often at no cost. What's more, hackathons are very popular, so that a good response is almost guaranteed. Some hackathons are confined to an organisation's or sector's own employees, but there is nothing to stop you from involving outsiders and experts, if that is what you want.

If you want to push through a change project that improves your organisation's relations with its customers, why not simply ask them in a hackathon where and how things can be improved? This will not only give you valuable information for your change trajectory, but also increase your ecosystem. If you can organise the hackathon as a game or competition, you will probably get an even bigger response, so that the boundary between your organisation and the outside world becomes blurred. In the past, I organised a few hackathons for banks that wanted to make banking more attractive for young people. With this in mind, we asked young people to take part in the event in return for a small reward. This worked extremely well and confirmed what I already knew: that hackathons are a powerful tool for collecting invaluable change data.

The power of rituals
—

" **Trying to push through a dry-as-dust change programme is asking for trouble. It is better to turn your trajectory into a brand. That increases people's feeling of involvement.**

Trying to push through a dry-as-dust change programme is asking for trouble. It is better to turn your trajectory into a brand. That increases people's sense of involvement. The most extensive changes usually have a programme, a name and a logo. This generates a campaign feeling. And if people feel that they are part of a campaign, you can stimulate feelings of pride and togetherness. I once had a client with a change trajectory that we decided to call Magellan. It was a good choice, because it sounds adventurous and makes it seem as though you are going on a voyage of discovery. Once you have created your brand, you need to get it promoted throughout the entire organisation. Distribute stylish images with the project logo, which can be used as backgrounds during online meetings. Dream up a few (but not too many) powerful hashtags that underline the feeling of togetherness. Yes, this is working with branding and status. Yes, these are essentially gimmicks – but your people will now feel part of the Magellan movement and they will like that feeling. Belonging to a club always feels good, because it gives both the illusion that you have been selected and the idea that you will contribute to something special. This works best if, as the leader, you can suggest that the proposed change is actually a part of the job. If people see change as an additional task, the project loses part of its strength.

In addition to branding, there are other marketing techniques that you will find useful during the change trajectory. The use of colours and aromas can influence human behaviour and that is precisely what you want to achieve as a change manager. Surprisingly, these techniques are still not widely used in change management, because much more attention is devoted to external communication rather than internal communication. A field of tension exists between these two forms of communication, in which they both compete for attention. Of course, the customer experience is extremely important, because at the end of the day it is the customer who pays, but who is it that provides the customer with that experience? Exactly: your own people. Not only those who are in direct contact with the customers, but also their other colleagues who support them by doing their jobs well. In other words, we are talking about something that touches the entire culture of the organisation. And as we have seen, the most difficult change trajectories are the ones that impact on an organisation's culture. Clarity and transparency in internal communication are therefore crucial.

This brings me back yet again to where we first started our story: the 'why' and the question of which kinds of change are easier or more difficult. Changing a culture is a fascinating process, but always involves a very difficult trajectory. In fact, it is almost as difficult as welding a blended family into a strong family unit. Tolerance and tension are the main ingredients. By using these to creating new rituals you can sometimes cross old boundaries and set new ones. A blended family can do this, for example, by going on holiday together. What did this used to be like in one family? What did it used to be like in the other family? What are we now going to do together? This can be a defining moment. Moral? Never underestimate the power of rituals.

At a certain moment, the coffee giant Starbucks started to use Workplace, a kind of Facebook for professionals. This made it possible for the CEO to communicate with the entire organisation via a video link. This is a powerful ritual, because everyone in the organisation occasionally likes to feel that they are in direct contact with the big boss. Discussing with your team what you do day in, day out is also a fun ritual, but there is a risk that it will become routine. Organisation-wide communication makes it possible to broaden and deepen the conversation to include inspirational matters like where we are going, where we can make the difference, what impact we have (and want to have) on society, and so on. In this way, you strengthen the organisation's sense of togetherness.

WALLS HAVE EARS

A technique that has been around for some time but is only now making its entrance into the world of change management is social listening. This technique assesses the level of popular feeling in the organisation. In a small company, the coffee machine is one of the most important places to apply this technique, because this is where people give vent to their feelings and discuss what is on their mind. Not only about their sick children or what they did at the weekend, but also about their work, their colleagues and their bosses. You can hear it all at the coffee machine! Now imagine that you have a thousand coffee machines at your disposal, all of them virtual. How would you collect all the details? And how do you decide which coffee machines and which data are more important or less important? This requires the use of sentiment analysis, in which software scans your internal communication for positive, neutral and negative sentiments. In e-mails, you can measure the balance between positive and negative words, but without reading the mail contents (because that would be a breach of the privacy legislation).

Consider, for example, the Magellan project that I mentioned in the paragraph above. It was possible to measure perfectly the extent to which communication about Magellan was positive or negative. This knowledge could then be used to make any necessary adjustments; for example, a new communication campaign that took better account of the field of tension between internal and external communication. In my experience, one of the main reasons for the frequent imbalance between these two forms of communication is the fact that external communication is usually outsourced to a professional communication bureau, whereas internal communication is allocated as an additional task to the organisation's own small communication team. This creates a distorted balance between the image of the change in the outside world and its perception inside the organisation. You have developed a strong and appealing campaign for the former, but failed to create the necessary momentum for it with the latter! That is a double missed opportunity. It is far better to allow the internal campaign to be shaped and implemented through the broad participation of your own people: that makes it three times as strong!

Don't become too efficient!
—

It is typical of human beings that they only understand and appreciate the importance of things once they are gone. This applies equally to rituals in a professional context. In this respect, the corona crisis was a good example. Because we were all required to work from home or at distance, we were suddenly cut off from human contact with our colleagues. During the first lockdown this was quite exciting, because the mysterious illness, at that time still shrouded in an aura of mystery, was dominating all our thoughts and actions, so that working from home was a blessing in disguise. But the longer we were forced to stay at home, the more we missed our regular place of work and the people we used to see every day. During team meetings, all we could now do was wave to each other, screen to screen, before quickly clicking on to the next meeting or getting back to the file we had called up online. As a result, during these years we have all become more efficient, because we no longer waste time talking at the coffee machine, walking from our office to the meeting room, and so on. Almost every form of dealing creatively with time and space has been eliminated. But if our work days have become more efficient, they have also been drained of their emotional content. As an employer, you can say that your employees now have an average of 45 fewer minutes of work each day and that you have given them this, almost like a present. However, this focuses purely on the functional aspects of the situation. Perhaps it is necessary to sometimes waste a few minutes in the course of a working day on light-hearted conversation and non-functional matters. If you can incorporate these things into the job, you turn them into a ritual. Twice each year, the Flemish television broadcaster VTM puts on a spectacular evening show for its stakeholders, such as shareholders, partners and the press. A galaxy of stars from the worlds of TV, film and music are drummed up to perform. On the afternoon before the gala, a dress rehearsal is held, to which all the VTM personnel are invited. This is a pure win-win operation, because the artists have a chance to try out their acts in situ and the staff get the feeling that they belong, that they are important to the organisation. In comparison, the few hours of lost working time are insignificant.

In this respect, the Colruyt supermarket chain has also developed an interesting dynamic. Colruyt is the least appealing Belgian supermarket in which to shop. The floor is made of concrete, the shelves are all in grey metal and there is little or no subsidiary decoration. However, Colruyt has one trump card that counteracts the effect of these drab surrounding: they have stands where you can try out new products and get a cup of coffee. During COVID, these stands were removed (understandably, for health reasons), but this was instantly big news on social media. The stands have now been returned, and this was also big news on social media. There is no other supermarket where you can shop more efficiently than Colruyt, but nobody talks about this or about the ugly store design. What they talk about is the coffee and the free samples. In fact, there is a good chance that these stands, which some might see as a waste of money, actually attract as many customers to Colruyt as the organisation's efficiency.

" If you have an organisational culture where trying out fun, new things and constantly learning from them is not encouraged, every change process will be a painful one.

Making your culture pleasanter and more enjoyable is not only important for your customers, but also for your personnel. In many American and Japanese companies the employees are provided with free meals at lunchtime and in the evening. 'Just so they can work for longer', you might think. Perhaps. But you can also see it positively: 'You are here, so we, the employer, might as well give you a decent meal.' Okay, it costs the company something, but this is more than offset by the gain in terms of a more attractive culture and greater staff engagement. I was once able to visit the Facebook campus in

San Francisco. There, they have even got an ice-cream salon distributing free ice-creams! There are lots of things of this kind that you can bring in to your organisational culture, all of which can contribute to what your personnel include in their psychological contract. Because this contract can vary from 'I do my job and work my agreed number of hours, but that's all' to 'I am interested to think about our work, contribute towards it, and work hard – sometimes too hard – to make it succeed'. Anything you can do to promote the latter at the expense of the former is a good thing and making this part of your change story can also be super-effective. Why? Because change itself is not efficient. There are always moments when you need to learn something new and that seldom runs smoothly at first. Even though you enjoy doing something new, it is more tiring, because you need to do it more consciously. Having to think about something is always difficult.

If you have an organisational culture where trying out fun, new things and constantly learning from them is not encouraged, every change process will be a painful one. This is a pity, because there is no reason why 'change' should be a dirty word. On the contrary: change is an inherent part of life. We are all different and we are all changing constantly: children, no children, small children, big children, no friends, lots of friends, closed doors, open doors, healthy periods, unhealthy periods, and so on. Life is, in fact, just one change after another, but this doesn't always give us a bad feeling. Okay, there are also bad changes, with illness and death at the top of the list. But most of the other changes are just a daily part of being alive. So why should we get so upset about change at work?

Toyota is one of the largest car constructors in the world. Since the company was first founded in 1937 by Kiichiro Toyoda, it has had a reputation for long-term thinking. Although the nature of their activity demands strong engineering in their systems, the autonomy of their employees has always been one of their central pillars. For example, it is widely known that at Toyota every worker is able to shut down the assembly line. This is something that for many years was unthinkable in American companies, but it attests to Toyota's remarkable dedication to quality and their desire to continually improve. This process is also a change in its own right, but at Toyota change has positive connotations for the entire workforce. This is important, because for most people change still has negative connotations. And if these people do not want to play along, nothing will change, no matter how many fine plans you make. But if you can create a context in which your personnel can also find something for themselves, based on the changes in what you do and how you do it, you will create a win-win situation that makes change possible.

For this reason, nowadays in change management we prefer to speak of 'transformation' rather than 'change', so that these negative connotations can be avoided. Transformation also lends itself more easily to pleasing imagery. Perhaps something along the lines of how a caterpillar becomes a butterfly? Brilliant, don't you think? Wrong! This would mean telling the workforce that they are currently ugly caterpillars and that clever old you is going to change them into beautiful butterflies. Two insults in a single sentence! No, you won't get very far that way. This demonstrates just how important symbols and words can be as part of the change process. Change also means that you are constantly building, no matter where you stand today. You are constantly building on the past, on the present and for the future. This is an evolutionary process that fosters and makes use of a growth mindset. But not everyone builds in the right way. Or builds at all. The most painful change is the change that you have overlooked for years and years. As a result, your organisation has become frozen, stuck in a rut where everyone is happy to rely further on the rights and the comfort that they have acquired over time. And now you want them to give it all up and change? Change in these circumstances feels like a slap in the face, not only in terms of your professional life but also privately. Faced with such a situation, resistance seems like the only possible answer. When this happens, your 'why', 'how' and 'what' become mixed up and lose their alignment. The only way out is to design your change as part of something that everyone will see as being beneficial – and fun.

COFFEE BREAK? HIGHLY RECOMMENDED!

Another technique that can be useful during the 'what' phase is the Net Promotor Score (NPS). This is a tool that measures customer loyalty and customer satisfaction. Whoever regularly buys things online will know: after you have received your order, you are asked to fill in a brief questionnaire. The key question relates to the extent to which you would be willing to recommend the services of the webshop to others. This is effectively a shortened version of the Net Promoter Score. The question usually asks you to give a score between 1 and 10. Whoever gives a score of 9 or 10 is willing to actively promote the product or service; a score of 4 or lower indicates complete dissatisfaction. Deducting the extremely negative scores from the extremely positive scores gives you the Net Promotor Score. This is the level of promotion that is actually being made. You can also use this technique as an employer to establish the extent to which your employees would recommend your organisation to potential job candidates. It is interesting to know this, precisely because it is a general feeling. It not only encompasses the nature of the work, but also the atmosphere amongst your personnel and even the quality of your coffee!

Renovation for beginners
—

To show how we can frame change positively, let us return briefly to the start of the 'what' phase. I described a change process as being like the game 'I go on holiday and I take with me…' If people in an organisation are wrestling with irritations, you can decide to leave those irritations behind. You give those people something else instead. Something positive that they can be a part of. In change processes there is an important distinction between the actors, who contribute towards the process, and the victims, who undergo the process. It is therefore the extent to which everyone can play an active role in the process that has a decisive impact on its nature and its likely success. If you simply undergo a change, if it is something that you must do, like it or not, you will not be happy and will most probably resist, or at least complain. This means that for leaders it is important to find the right balance between contributing and undergoing. Obviously, it would be difficult to ask every employee every week how the organisation can change for the better, but there are small things that you can do at team level which will have a positive effect.

If, for example, you work in a shift system, there is always a handover moment between shifts. I mentioned earlier how important it is to do something more than simply hand over the key; namely, to also give a summary of what went well and what went wrong during the previous shift. On first hearing, this might sound dry and functional, but you can actually turn it into a learning moment. For instance, you can explain how and why the machines have been set up in a particular way and what consequences this might have for the new shift. If you liaise with each other again later on – not just about current status but also for the purposes of anticipation – you develop an interactive process in which a sense of responsibility can gradually grow. This adds a new dimension to the handover moment: 'How do I transfer the shift to you and how do you transfer it back to me?' You can create a similar dynamic in public spaces that you hire. This also involves a kind of transfer and therefore is also an interactive process. Are the rooms clean or not when you rent them? Are the rooms clean or not when you hand them back? This forms the basis for the interaction. Depending on the answer, you can either foster a relationship of confidence and trust that strengthens you both, or else descend into in a negative spiral that serves no one's interests.

For me, this human dynamic is one of the most fascinating elements in all change processes, but, ironically enough, it is also the element that is most frequently overlooked by organisations. When company leaders announce change, most of the employees respond with a deep sigh, even if only because of the nature of the announcement. To make matters worse, many companies like to announce more than one change at the same time, so that the sigh gets deeper and deeper. Many leaders see this as unwillingness to cooperate, whereas in reality it is a logical human dynamic. Imagine that you would do the same thing in your private life. Let's say, for example, that you are renovating your kitchen. You can approach this in different ways, but you know that whatever you do there will inevitably be a number of inconveniences. Most people stay in the house during the work and find another way to cook and to cope with the other daily irritations. If, however, you decide to renovate the bathroom at the same time, these irritations will start to pile up. Now you can no longer make your bacon and eggs or have a shower! If both these things are important to you, your day will get off to a really bad start. Deep sighs all round! And it is the same at the organisational level. People can deal with one change, even if it causes them inconvenience. But two changes at the same time is too much for most organisations to bear. This is something of which company leaders are not sufficiently aware.

Moreover, these leaders also view change at the abstract level, without taking account of the concrete context. For example, the length of a first change programme is estimated at one month, and so they plan to launch a second one immediately afterwards. This is much too soon, especially in organisations where the support for change is far from unanimous. But even in other organisations there is always a chance that the first programme will overrun as a result of the concrete context, so that the two programmes will overlap. Just like when you are planning to renovate both your kitchen and your bathroom, it is better to leave a gap between them: the work might be more complex than you thought and perhaps some of the contractors will fail to turn up as promised. Of course, it is simply not possible in an organisation to consult with your personnel about every decision: that would result in an absurd democratic process that would bring everything to a grinding halt. For this reason, I am a big fan of cooperative companies, where different elements are brought together for a collaborative enterprise. In this way, you get a fantastic balance between independence and collectivity. You get a similar dynamic in a partnership model, in which the partners experience their interaction at an even more conscious level. By comparison, the balance in the relationship between employer and employer is, in my opinion, often very unhealthy. But that is another story.

One of the reasons why the human dynamic is often overlooked is that most organisations are not structured around the experience of its human workforce but focus instead on a different logic, such as activity domains, functional domains or even geographical locations. These domains share a common factor: they do not treat people as people. Even the personnel department does not treat people as people, regarding them simply as just one of various anonymous factors they have to deal with. True, you are a person at the moment you sign your contract, when you are paid at the end of the month, or when you register for a training programme, but these are just fragments, whereas the experience of an employee should be a whole. When you look back over the previous week, do you have a generally good feeling or a generally bad one? Details certainly help to determine that feeling, but it is the overall impression that counts. As an employee, you are also partly responsible for that feeling, by identifying what you have done well and where you have made a difference. Some people do this every day; others do it once every six months; some never do it at all. But by doing it properly and consistently, it is possible to make the employee experience measurable. Hence the comparison I made earlier with Start to Run. If the employees in a change trajectory know their objectives and can monitor their progress towards them, this will result in a positive endorsement of that trajectory.

The Silent Language

In *The Silent Language*, the American anthropologist Edward T. Hall looks at the power of silence as part of language. He also examines how people in different cultures use space. If we in the West are in a hotel lobby or waiting room, we generally try to find a corner or another spot where we will feel comfortable. When a second person enters, he or she will choose a position in relation to the first person, with the aim of keeping as much distance as possible. But it is completely different in Arab cultures. In this case, the second person will take up a position as close as possible to the first or will even try to persuade him or her to give up the seat, if it is a better one. This unspoken language is fascinating and can be used to great effect in change management and, above all, negotiations.

Edward T. Hall, Bantam, 1973

Talking to the crows
—

At the end of the 'what' phase, we have at our disposal sufficient instruments and tactics to translate the change as concretely and as tangibly as possible. We started with an abstract idea, because that in essence is what change is, and we are now able to put that idea into practice. It is this abstract nature of change ideas that makes things so difficult for change consultants like myself.

Imagine that an organisation approaches me with the idea that they want their employees to live more healthily. This sounds good, but is highly abstract. How do you translate this abstraction into the daily lives of the employees? Who are these employees and what are their own opinions about living healthily? For example, it is reasonable to expect that the employees should not remain seated for more than one hour without the opportunity to move about. So how do you proceed? You can mention this in a personnel meeting, but thereafter no one will do much about it. Or you can work with alarm signals, such as sport watches that encourage people to take a certain number of steps each hour. Or you could say that from now on no meeting will last for more than 50 minutes. Of course, this is only one aspect of the situation. Living more healthily could also mean giving people a number of free 'off-days': days when they can stay at home when they are not feeling good. This system exists in the Netherlands and is a fantastic idea, which has proven its worth by eliminating many sources of irritation and reducing the level of burn-out. By contrast, when you are feeling off colour, in some countries you have to visit a doctor to get a sick note, but this is not always easy if you do not have a valid medical problem. Not feeling motivated is certainly a problem, but it is not one that a doctor can assess by sticking a motivation thermometer under your tongue. As a result, you have to go into work, even though you are feeling rotten, because taking a free 'off-day' is not an option. Conclusion? The more concrete and more varied the employer makes the range of options, the greater the possibility for the individual employees to make their own choices about the best way to live more healthily.

For me, allowing people to make their own choices and creating a human dynamic to encourage behavioural change is the essence of every change trajectory. You give people the necessary levers to exercise influence on the quality of their own work and lives. This makes the margin for change much greater, because most changes in a work environment are not fundamental. There are very few people who wake up in the morning as a plumber and decide that from tomorrow onwards they would like to be a pilot. That is a fundamental change, even transformational. And there is a huge difference. My friend and HR director Ivo Pareyns expresses it as follows: 'Change management is something you do every day, to a greater or lesser extent. With a transformation, at the end you have something totally different from what you started with.

Many companies like to say that they engage in change management, but in reality all they are doing is what I call crow management. If a horde of crows are sitting in a tree and you clap your hands, the crows will go and sit on a different branch of the same tree. For me, change management is often like that in many organisations: you think that you have changed something but almost everything remains the same. With a transformation, you cut down the tree and plant a new one. Or even a whole forest.' Most changes are not transformational. They only impinge on a part of what you do. If you decide to become a vegan, you cannot do it for just two meals a week. You are either a vegan or you aren't. You can, however, first become a flexitarian, so that you can gradually build up to becoming a vegan. How clear do organisations make choices of this kind? They should be as clear as possible – because that is the key to success.

> **" Allowing people to make their own choices and creating a human dynamic to encourage behavioural change is the essence of every change trajectory.**

If an organisation wants to cut costs because the owner wants to make a bigger profit, that is a legitimate reason. The question is then whether or not, as a leader, you communicate this intention transparently and consistently, or do you try to develop a more attractive story that camouflages the real reason for the change? Next, you create a design to show how you will make your planned savings and how your people will be expected to deal with them. Will you go for a high level of participation and devise flexible programmes or will you simply issue an instruction saying that, for example, everyone needs to make a saving of 5 percent, on the assumption that 5 percent does not sound very much and everyone will have the feeling that it is feasible? Most companies opt for the 'cuts-across-the-board' approach, with everyone doing everything with a little bit less. But trying to save 5 percent on everything in an organisation is both perverse and absurd. Because what happens then? One team leader is committed to the organisation and has been working economically for years, whereas another team leader is less committed and has been wasting cash extravagantly. But now they are both expected to save the same amount! For one of them, that is a drama; for the other, it is a joke. No, it is much better to cut costs in a targeted manner and, above all, to devise a method of implementation that allows the teams themselves to decide where savings can be made. Once again, this involves making a reasoned choice between the imposition of rules and the encouragement of principles. This is a field of tension that you will need to confront throughout the change trajectory, up to and including the 'what' phase: do you give your people rules that will allow them to play the game for themselves or do you play the game for them? This choice, and the mix on which you eventually decide, is the most fascinating aspect of the entire change story: the intention, the guidelines, the instructions and the space for human behaviour. For me, that is what change is all about. And as I said right from the very start: it really is child's play.

Loop after loop after loop

We have now come to the end of our figure-of-eight loop. Did we cross the finishing line together? And have we both won? Or do we still need the help of someone else before we can win? These are the first questions that come to mind at this moment. It is important to notice that the emphasis is on 'together'. Take another look at the lists of questions at the start of each chapter

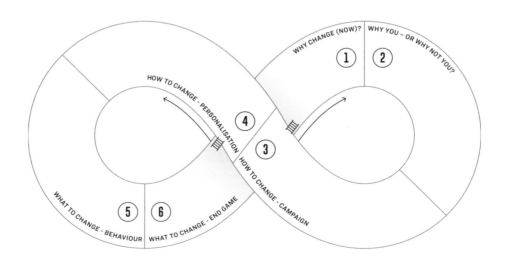

and try to spot the difference. Exactly: all the lists contain 'you' questions, except the final chapter, which contains 'we' questions. This is a crucial point that you should never forget in any process or change trajectory: in an organisation you do nothing alone; an organisation is always about the interaction of people.

The next question that deserves an honest answer is this: was your 'why' worth all the effort? You then need to carry this answer with you into your following change trajectory or the other trajectories that are running concurrently. My friend Tony Bradshaw, CEO of Allianz Benelux, like to compare this with climbing a mountain. 'A long succession of changes or a status quo between two turbulent processes? Many companies are confronted by both. One department can stay in the base camp for a while, while the other starts climbing. One department takes years to get up a gentle slope, while another can climb steep ascents almost from the word "go". But many companies are never given the option to build a base camp for a temporary status quo. They need to change continually, either through the pressure of outside influences or because of the nature of the organisation. As long as you know what forms of change are necessary and can separate them from each other in a manner that allows them to coexist, there is no problem. But if they cannot exist alongside each other in the type of company that you run, then you do indeed have a problem. And this brings us back to the nature of the change, which is where everything starts.'

Every change trajectory can generate goodwill and badwill, and this is something that you also need to take with you into the future. And remember that every change will also change you as a leader. It can boost your image and status or it can give them a serious knock. At the same time, it can also bring you greater self-knowledge and new insights. This is something else that you need to weigh up when you come to the end of the loop. And because our loop is endless, you can probably all guess what the final question is going to be. So, are you ready to play another game?

LITERATURE

Beer, Michael & Nohria, Nitin, *Breaking the Code of Change* (Harvard Business School Press, 2000).

Braun, Danielle & Kramer, Jitske, *The Corporate Tribe: Organizational Lessons From Anthropology* (Routledge, 2016).

De Vries, Manfred Kets, *Seks & geld, geluk en dood* (Palgrave, 2009).

Dweck, Carol S., *Mindset* (SWP, 2018).

Edmondson, Amy C., *The Fearless Organization* (Wiley, 2018).

Fisher, Roger & Shapiro, Daniel, *Beyond Reason: Using Emotions as You Negotiate* (Penguin Putnam Inc, 2006).

Gibbons, Paul, *The Science of Successful Organizational Change* (Pearson Education, 2015).

Gino, Francesca, *Rebel Talent* (Del Rey Street Books, 2018).

Goffee, Robert & Jones, Gareth, *Why Should Anyone Be Led by You? What It Takes To Be an Authentic Leader* (Harvard Business School Press, 2006).

Hall, Edward T., *The Silent Language* (Bantam, 1973).

Herrero, Leandro, *Viral Change* (Memphis State University Press, 2008)

Hutton, Wendy, *Singapore Food* (Times, 1979).

Inamori, Kazuo, *Amoeba Management* (CRC Press, 2012).

Kahneman, Daniel, *Thinking, fast and slow* (Farrar, Straus & Giroux Inc, 2013).

Kellerman, Barbara, *The End of Leadership* (Harvard Businesss School Press, 2012).

Kotter, John, *Leading Change* (Harvard Business School Press, 2012).

Laloux, Frederic, *Reinventing Organizations* (Diateino, 2015).

Lewin, Kurt, *Field Theory of Learning* (Harper & Brothers, 1951).

Lewin, Kurt, *Resolving Social Conflicts* (American Psychological Association, 1997).

Macchiavelli, Niccolò, *De vorst* (Athenaeum, 2019).

McChrystal, Stanley A., *Team of Teams: New Rules of Engagement for a Complex World* (Penguin Books Ltd, 2015).

Murray, Douglas, *The Madness of the Crowds: Gender, Race and Identity* (Bloomsbury Publishing, 2019).

Senge, Peter, *The Fifth Discipline* (Random House Books, 2015).

Senge, Peter, *The Necessary Revolution* (Currency, 2010).

Stengel, Richard, *Nelson Mandela: 15 lessen over leven, liefde en leiderschap* (Kosmos, 2010).

Sun Tzu, *De kunst van het oorlogvoeren* (Librero 2000).

Taylor, Frederick Winslow, *The Principles of Scientific Management* (Dover Publications, 2003).

Thaler Richard H. & Sunstein Cass R., *Nudge: Improving Decisions About Health, Wealth, and Happiness* (Yale University Press, 2008).

Weick, Karl E. & Sutcliffe, Kathleen M., *Managing the Unexpected* (Wiley, 2015).

ACKNOWLEDGEMENTS

──────

THIS BOOK IS THE RESULT of a thought process that has lasted for years, with a constant reshaping and repolishing of ideas. But it is also the result of countless meetings with clients, colleagues and friends. I would like to thank everyone who has crossed my path at one time or another and who in that way has enriched not only my ideas but also my life. In particular, I would like to thank Anthony Bradshaw, Ivo Pareyn and Alix Rombouts for their contributions to this book, and also my room-filling friend Paul Gibbons for his refreshing insights.

Finally, a special word of thanks also goes to Niels Janssens and Marije Roefs at LannooCampus, Steven Theunis and Thijs Kestens from the Armée de Verre Design Studio and David Janssens from Het Woordkantoor, for the great enthusiasm with which he was able to bring order to my sometimes turbulent ideas, without losing any of their meaning.